A New Testament Trilogy

Our God

Ourselves

Our Community

A Journey of Radical Discovery

Tom Johnston
Mike Chong Perkinson

The Praxis Center For Church Development
PO Box 4878
Manchester, NH 03108
www.praxiscenter.org

Published by ChurchSmart Resources

We are an evangelical Christian publisher committed to producing excellent products at affordable prices to help church leaders accomplish effective ministry in the areas of church planting, church growth, church renewal and leadership development.

For a free catalog of our resources call 1-800-253-4276.

A New Testament Trilogy

Our God

Ourselves

Our Community

INDEX

ACKNOWLEDGEMENTS

To our wives

From Tom — *Cathy, thank you for working fulltime to support my church planting habit, for your partnership with me in the Harvest Community and for releasing me to this thing called Praxis. The Father has taught me so much through you – about friendship and community, about grace and mercy, about determination and resilience. You truly are the embodiment of Jesus' love, acceptance and forgiveness. If there was a Proverbs 32, it would be about you. I love you.*

From Mike — *Teresa, you are the anchor our Father has used to help me understand and appreciate the reality of family and community. Thank you for being such a great partner in ministry, friend, and the love of my life. Your release and support have increased my love for Jesus. I am honored to do community with you as we share the love of our Father with each other. I love you with my life. And of course, to the second most important girl in my life, Sierra, daddy loves you!*

To our mentors

We would thank those people in our lives that have shaped us in Christ:

To Dr. Bob Logan — *Thank you for setting us on this path we share together in this thing called Praxis. (We understand if we are captured that you will disavow any knowledge of our actions.)*

Tom would like to thank Glenn Moon, Dr. David Schieber and Rev. Leo Sauve'.

Mike would like to thank Don Smith and the late Dr. William L. Lane.

To our proofreaders

Thanks to Marjorie Clark, Donna Fry, Catherine Maillet, Jodie McCay, and Lorna Miller for wading through the pages of this book. (We hope the prayer, counseling and medication will help you recover!)

Those we live in community with

Special thanks to the Harvest Community in New Hampshire and Living Hope in California. You make our lives rich with Jesus.

Cover Art

The Trinity Knot, this one with an Alpha Omega in the pattern, is an ancient Celtic symbol for the Trinity. Thanks to Cari Buziak for the artwork.

FOREWORD

As the popular folk song reminds us, "The times, they are a-changing." What has worked in the past, won't necessarily work today. While writing this preface, I am reminded of how culture, society, traditions and technology are constantly shifting. Technological advances allow me to email, instant message and create a manuscript all on my wireless laptop while sitting in an airport or a local café. However, 20 years ago I would have been tied to my desk, writing on my new word processor and communicating with my publisher by phone and a two-day courier service.

Technology has also impacted our sense of community. Like many of us in today's culture, I can go an entire day without seeing the face of anyone other than a family member. My colleagues and I at CoachNet International Ministries all work from home, communicating through email and the Internet. On some days, there is no need to venture outside or even connect with someone in person. Gone are the days when people sat on the front porch and visited with neighbors and friends. The term "community" has a different meaning in today's society, particularly with current and future generations.

Sociologists say that the emerging generations — the Xers and Millenials — crave community, that their commitment to one another and their bonds of friendship are unlike that of other generations. Because of technology, their community can include anyone around the world, but their need for relation-ships, to know and be known, is a God-given desire the He has placed in all generations.

Tom Johnston and Mike Chong Perkinson address these issues and other important concerns relevant to the church and community in *A New Testament Trilogy — Our God, Ourselves and Our Community*. They are church planting and ministry leaders who I've known for many years. They think biblically, strategically, and practically — and they are keenly aware of the value of relationships with God, others and ourselves. This book is designed around the importance of thinking fundamentally about who God is...whowe are... and how we relate to one another in community. Tom and Mike's insights flow out of the crucible of experience, empowering readers like you to prayerfully and strategically shape your ministry in a way that will produce transformation in your life and that of those with whom you relate.

Moving into new waters takes courage and involves learning as you go. We all know that putting a band-aid on an issue does not solve the problem. Anything as important as developing community in and outside of your church needs to be thoroughly studied and examined. The questions at the end of each chapter will help you learn to think your way into a new way of acting… and act your way into a new way of thinking.

I invite you join the quest and take the journey. Read carefully, reflect prayerfully and act courageously. I am very pleased to be in community with Tom and Mike and I know this book is a very important resource that will help church leaders meet the challenge of today's world.

Dr. Robert E. Logan
Los Angels, California

INTRODUCTION

We are, by God's grace, in the process of rediscovering the truth of the New Testament Scriptures.

This book, this Trilogy, is about a journey of radical rediscovery. Rooted in the ancient and sacred text of the Holy Scripture, our path of rediscovery takes us through many crossings, on a pilgrimage of heart and mind as we seek a fresh encounter with God. Our hearts, like many that we have conversed with, ache for the fullness of what it means to be a child of God, living the life of glory, truth, and grace so powerfully expressed in the life of Jesus. There is nothing that reflects the glory of God more than human beings who are fully alive in Christ.

We are not suggesting that we have found a new truth about God, us, or the Church, but that we are rediscovering what the Bible has been saying for centuries. Somewhere in our journey we took a wrong turn and ended up at a dead end. A place where boredom and frustration reign and the joy and power of God have no place.

Our travels through several key biblical concepts are more than just a review. It is rediscovery. On our trek together, we will see vistas familiar to our heart — we know that they are there — but many have been long absent from our mind, our life and our ministry. We also hope to encounter blazing new horizons of understanding as the Holy Spirit shines His light on us, and in us.

However, our quest that forms the core of our expedition is not just *to know*, but it is also *to be known*. Our journey is not one that is ruled by a desire to simply acquire more *information*, but rather we seek *transformation*. We desire life to emerge more fully in us, changing us into His likeness. We pray that in this journey you find life imparted to you rather than a new way to package the principles of Scripture or church growth (some new tips and techniques). As wonderful as information is, without the impartation of life from above, it is nothing but mere human effort that seeks to create something divine and meaningful. As noble as such a task might be without the power of God the Holy Spirit, it simply will not happen nor feed the devastating hunger in the human soul.

Our path starts with our Creator, as we revisit the core issues in the understanding of **Our God**. From there our trail will wind through God's Word as we look at **Ourselves**, seeking a clearer view of our identity as sons and daughters, servants and stewards. Our journey will wind up in the refreshing oasis of **Our Community**, as we see how the Father forms us together into a Kingdom community that reflects the brilliance of His image to those trapped in a darkened world.

But the journey doesn't end there — the road continues ever onward as our rediscovery begins to touch not just our life, but also our ministry praxis. It affects how we make disciples, and how we develop leaders for the body of Christ. It determines how we will facilitate the emergence of pastoral leaders from within our communities. It forms the larger framework on how God builds healthy and effective wineskins — local churches — to reap and keep a harvest of souls. Our exploration of rediscovery even informs how we multiply those wineskins in ever-increasing numbers, gathering more and more people into the community of the King.

On a personal note — You will find much of this book discusses the idea of community at varying levels, based within the nature of the Trinity, community's effect on the identity of the human individual and how the greatest expression of the Church is to reflect God as, and through being, community.

We have found that even in writing this book, and the associated developmental experiences and tools which flow from it, that it was impossible for us to write without living community itself. This posed certain issues as we live on opposite North American coasts — Tom on the East Coast of the United States, and Mike on the West Coast. Finding that God literally gave us "writer's block" unless we were together interacting, we have flown back and forth across the country as part of our quest, being forced to live out the interdependence of community in the pursuit of this work. Apart from Him in each other, we could do nothing. Together in Him, we found we could do all things. Having written many things in the past as individuals "on our own," we at first found the God-imposed inability frustrating and confusing. Once we figured out what He was doing to us, we realized again a profound sense of awe about the peculiar sovereignty of our brotherhood in Him, being both humbled and exhilarated by what the Lord was doing. Besides, we racked up some serious frequent flyer and hotel points!

To you, the reader, our companions on this quest, we pray that the words on these pages will be used by God to both inspire and prepare. We hope they inspire you to explore further down the path of rediscovery, and prepare you for your journey. We hope these pages will empower you to see, taste, touch, hear and smell the fresh reality of church which we believe the New Testament brings to our times. May the Holy Spirit illuminate His path in your heart and mind as you step out on this adventure.

Tom Johnston
Mike Chong Perkinson

PART 1

Our God

CHAPTER 1

"GOD IS ONE"

God — a word that triggers a sense of mystery and fond affection and yet, a word that is difficult to fully wrap our minds around. Giving definition and explanation to our Creator is no easy task. In one sense, attempting to describe God is as much an exercise of excessive analogy as it would be to explain infinity. Just how do we explain a concept that eludes the finite human mind? As difficult as this might be, it is, nonetheless, important for us to understand the nature of God. That is, who He is. If the assumption is true that what we do flows from who we are, then it must be true of all beings, including God. Just as the genetic code of DNA is vital to the formation of a human being — there is always a basis by which form is given substance — it is important to grasp what might be the DNA of our God. God is the basis or foundation of our universe and it finds its form and expression through Him, the One who holds all things together (Acts 17:28; with reference to Christ, Colossians 1:15-18). Since God is the creator of all that is, it would be important for us to understand the nature of our Creator. This understanding would provide the basis of our faith, theology, ecclesiology, relationships, etc.

As a matter of fact, our understanding of God already influences our faith, theology, ecclesiology, relationships, etc. How we view God has a great deal to do with determining our theological constructs and our ecclesiological practices. Christian A. Schwarz goes so far as to say, "In my opinion, the widespread lack of understanding of the God who reveals himself in a three-fold way is the main reason for the shocking paralysis of vast sectors of Christianity. It also explains why we Christians have been dealing with the challenges confronting us in the new millennium." (*The Threefold Art of Experiencing God: The Liberating Power of a Trinitarian Faith*, ChurchSmart Resources: St. Charles, IL, 1999, p. 4.)

What distinguishes Christianity from other religions is the nature of a personal God who comes to us as God the Father, God the Son, and God the Holy Spirit. There is no other religious teaching that provides us with such an all-powerful Being that is at once so transcendent and immanent. The God who stands over and above the created order as something wholly "Other" and yet, so close, "Immanuel" ("God with us," Matthew 1:23), that He can live in our hearts. It is a dialectic that cannot be resolved and any attempt to do so will result in either a limited view of God that makes him distant (reducing Him to a cosmic force) or "Other" or a heretical understanding of God that makes Him in our image. The apostle Paul brings these polarities together (synthesis) for us in Ephesians 4:6:

There is only one God and Father, who is over us all and in us all and living through us all.

God is then wholly "Other," and yet a personal God that lovingly involves Himself with His creation as the Incarnation (John 1:14) so powerfully illus-trated.

It is primarily the distinctive of a personal God who comes to us as God the Father, God the Son, and God the Holy Spirit that needs to be central in our understanding to the Christian faith. It is our estimation that a great deal of our struggle with our faith, theology, ecclesiology, and practice is a result of a misunderstanding of who God is. A misunderstanding of God's nature can only lead to a misunderstanding of ourselves and our roles as pastors and leaders. John Calvin made it quite clear that proper self-knowledge can only come through a proper knowledge of God. Knowing God is then pivotal and critical in knowing ourselves. All doctrinal constructs are built upon the foun-dation of one's view of God and the self.

Simply, life is nothing more than relationship. First our relationship with God (the Ultimate, the "Thou" by which the "I" of self is known). Second, our relationship with ourselves. And third, our relationship with others. It is the first, our relationship with God that informs and shapes the other two relation-ships. As we find ourselves in God, then our relationship with ourselves becomes whole. Our fragile human self can only become complete when it is built upon the foundation that gives us definition and purpose. It is when we find ourselves in God that we find the ability to love others as whole beings as we have been loved by the One who makes us whole (I John 4:19, "We love because He first loved us."). When our relationship with God is right, then in Christ, love has the potential to move from a self-centered love to an other-centered love.

Let us explain: God loves us like Beauty loved the Beast (the great fairy tale made into a Walt Disney classic). There was nothing beautiful about the Beast that caused Beauty to love him. Rather it was her love that made him beautiful. Unconditional love does not mean that God loves us and it does not matter what we do, rather it means that there is nothing in us that draws Him to us. *Eros* love is that love which is aroused when one sees beauty in another and loves the beauty within them. This is not to say such love is wrong, but to simply describe the love that is most familiar to humanity. *Agape* love, God's unconditional love, is the love that loves because God is love. In other words, God loves us not because we are beautiful — there is nothing in Him that needs anything. Rather He gives love to us and it is His love that makes us beautiful. And so, unconditional love is that love that is given to us by God that is based on Him and not us. Which means His love will never change because there was nothing we could to do to gain it and nothing we can do to lose it. Finding ourselves in God will allow us to become whole persons expressing His love more fully as he originally designed.

Since our understanding of God already influences our faith, theology, ecclesiology and relationships, maybe this is why our differing theological positions can never fully be resolved. For one thing, they are too personal. Frederick Buechner stated, "All theology is autobiography." At first glance one might consider such a statement heretical or extreme (Solipsism, which is the theory that it is only the self that can be known and verified). But after some reflection, we believe Buechner has hit upon a truth that is often overlooked. As we develop and process our theologies there is an autobiographical reality that comes into play. What we say about God is often a reflection of how we view ourselves. This is not to say that all theology is based on the self, a creating God in our own image, as Ludwig Feuerbach (and later his follower Karl Marx) accused Christianity of projecting its own, worldly images onto heaven and calling that self-created being God. Rather, it is to say that the theological journey is a personal one. We are discovering ourselves as we discover God.

As a result, our differing theological positions often flow from a personal misunderstanding of God and ourselves, causing us to focus on one aspect (or polarity–like transcendence) of God over and often, against another (polarity–like immanence). Like the right and left parts of our brain, providing opposite but necessary functions, is it possible that our theological variances, in many cases, were never meant to be brought together? Rather than posing one aspect of God against the other, as we so often do, a synthesis of sorts might be the answer to our dilemma. After all, God is transcendent (beyond us, the "Other") and He is immanent (remaining in creation, within reach, in our hearts). Of course we are not suggesting that any incorrect view of God should be allowed to remain and synthesized into a whole — an error mixed with truth does not make truth — but we are arguing that our extreme misunderstandings of God are often centered around an incorrect under-standing of who God is. That is, our need to polarize often results in a God that is far from what the Scripture and the Incarnation reveal. As we have noted, our earthly existence supports the reality of polarities existing side by side, which if synthesized bring fullness. Simply, God is both "beyond us" and near, "in our hearts." The polarities bring a fullness that helps us see the whole, or in this case see God for who He really is. Just the simple declara-tion in the relational world of men and women supports this. As it is often said, "opposites attract."

Now let us take you down a path that is often the most misunderstood and even avoided topic within the Christian faith. The idea that the One God meets us in three persons is considered to be among the most opaque and least accessible doctrines of all Christian theology. As slippery as this teaching might be, the Scriptures imply it on almost every page. God then eternally exists as one God in three persons, Father, Son, and Holy Spirit, and each person is fully God. Maybe it is safe to assert here that our attempt to explain the doctrine of the Trinity is more pragmatic than abstract or theoret-ical. The aim of this chapter is not to develop another theological treatise on the Trinity but to simply come to a clear understanding of God's nature — one God in three persons — which will assist us when it comes to processing the realities of human nature (ourselves) and the church (our communities). Exactly what is it that God desires of us as His people and His church in rela-tionship to who He is?

The word "Trinity" is never found in the Bible, though the concept is taught throughout Scripture. Augustine believed that God left triune footprints throughout the created order (God's DNA, if you will). Everything seems to point to this mystery (Augustine, *On The Trinity*. VIII. 10, *The Nicene & Post-Nicene Fathers* 1 III, p. 124; IX, pp. 125ff.; X.17-19, pp. 134-143). One of Augustine's many analogies utilized love which requires a lover, one who is loved, and the love that unites them, in a kind of three-in-oneness and yet, still speaking only of one thing, love. We find these hints of God's triune nature all throughout creation. There is something about the nature of God that suggests that unity and diversity are part of the fabric of creation. Again, polarities exist and must be allowed to co-exist side by side (synthesized into a whole) for us to grasp the fullness of who God is and who we are in Him.

God is then a tri-unity, three-in-one, or triune. That is, one God and yet, three persons of Father, Son, and Holy Spirit. God is not an impersonal personal power source by which the known universe is held together. According to Scripture God is not a cosmic "it" that ebbs and flows in power surges that randomly create, and, out of some magnificent ordering of chaos, gives birth to what we know now as human life. God is a person. There is something about the divine nature that is relational and communal that must be understood and experienced by those in Christ.

As we have noted, understanding the nature of the God we serve is an important endeavor. Like all fields of study, we enter our domain with presuppositions already in place, methodologies ready to be employed, and in some cases, pre-judgments already made. For example, the Trinitarian theologies of the Christian West and Christian East differ in emphasis. The West places its highlight on the unity of the divine essence, whereas the East on the triplicity of the divine persons. Presuppositions or pre-understandings clearly impact our conclusions and even at times limit them. It is of interest to note how the Catholic comes to Matthew 16 with a presupposition that Christ is referring to Peter as the "rock" or first pope of a long line of popes to come from the church in Rome. On the other hand, the Protestant comes to the text, already pre-determining the meaning of the text as Christ making reference to the declaration of Peter as the "rock" upon which the Church will be built. Our presuppositions guide our interpretations and methodologies. If our presuppositions of God are not correct or complete, then the working out of our theology will be at best rather dismal or lifeless.

Rather than debate the various implications of Trinity that have been provided throughout our rich history, we seek to stand on the shoulders of those who have gone before us so that we might be able to view the horizon a little more clearly. The church fathers that gathered for the Council of Chalcedon in 451 a.c.e., were able to provide a language that would allow the

Church to speak about the Trinity. From the composite wisdom, led by the Holy Spirit, they were able to give us a language that would allow us to describe the Trinity and set parameters for what is orthodox and what is not. In other words, God is one and yet three persons. He is not one God who has three modes of operation. Modalism, Sabellianism, and Dynamic Monarchianism all taught a variance of one being with three different ways to express himself (same God with three suits or outfits he wears of Father, Son, and Holy Spirit). God is not three modes or three gods. He is one God in three persons.

The finite human mind comes up empty here, like the hand trying to grasp air. Just because the hand cannot grasp air does not mean it's not there. We feel its effects and see its movements — the wind leaves it finger-prints everywhere. Just because we cannot get our mental hand around the concept does not mean it is wrong or that God does not exist as Trinity. It is not a contradiction, but a mystery — something that is larger than us. One might be able to explain the "Big Bang" theory, but not the origin of the universe. There may have been an explosion, but how did the matter that exploded get here? Science eventually comes up empty and turns to theology or philosophy for explanations regarding the origin of things. There are things all over our universe that leave us dumbfounded and pondering the greater mystery of existence. Mystery is all around us. Science has tried its best to reduce mystery to equations, theories, and axioms, but the more it tries the more it seems to uncover mystery.

It is important for us to let the mystery exist. We believe with the historic Christian faith that God is all-powerful, the Creator of everything, three persons; each person is fully God; and God is one. He is within Himself a relational community of three persons: Father, Son, and Holy Spirit. The relational aspects of the created order (God's DNA) give us clues as to God's nature and design for the human race and for our purposes, the Church.

With great reverence and humility, we now will attempt to explain this mystery.

CHAPTER 2

"GOD IS TRINITY: A COMMUNITY"

We have thus far been contending that God exists as one God in three persons. If we are correct in our understanding that God exists as a relational being who exists in love with each member of the Trinity and shares and extends that love to his creation ("Let Us make people in our image", Genesis 1:26), then it will have an enormous impact on our spirituality and ecclesiology and every other "ology" you can come up with.

In progressive revelation revealed in the Old Testament we find the foundation for the fuller expression of the God in three persons found in the New Testament. It has been said that "the Old is in the New concealed; the New is the Old revealed." The plural pronouns (Genesis 1:26 "Let Us make people in our image, to be like ourselves" and Genesis 11:7 "Come, let's go down and give them different languages") help us see that God is one who subsists as three eternal and co-equal persons. There are a variety of other passages that distinguish the person of God (Yahweh and Adonai in Psalm 110:1) and the Ancient of Days and the Son of Man in Daniel 7:9-14.

The logical conclusion, the DNA factor, since God made us in His image and likeness, is that we have been created to exist as persons in relationship to Him and each other as a community that is both one and diverse. We have become members (through the atoning work of Christ; Luke 22:20) of the new covenant community that is called to reflect the glory of the Godhead in His corporate unity (John 17:22-26). God's redemptive plan is to restore relationships at every level — with God, self, others, and creation — so that we will find ourselves living in the *shalom* (peace, love, unity, harmony) of the Trinity.

Let us now take a moment to clarify our discussion about the one God in three persons as we look at God's nature as one (being) and his function or roles (economy) as three persons.

Ontological View: The joy of any theological discussion is the use of words that create a dynamic tension for the mind. You know, a headache that often results in frustrating the reader to the point of confusion or even boredom. At best, it is often difficult to ascertain the connection between such theoretical and abstract doctrines to our church practice and lives. We are well aware of this risk and hope to limit this as much as possible.

When we speak of ontological we are dealing with the aspect of "being". And by so doing we are attempting to speak about God as He is within Himself. We will not take much of our time to do this since such discussion is nearly impossible to digest by the finite mind. As a matter of fact, if you totally grasp this explanation of the Trinity then it is more than likely that we have created a heresy. Heresies regarding the Trinity make rational and under-standable a mystery that cannot be grasped by the human mind. As we have already noted, we seek to let the mystery remain without any tampering on our part. The danger in any discussion of the Trinity is to over analogize and turn God into something we can fully comprehend. This is not to say the doctrine of the Trinity is irrational or incomprehensible, but that we are talking about realities that are infinite and beyond a finite mind to fully understand. The doctrine of Trinity, we must assert, is a description of God as He is in Himself and as He has revealed Himself to us. The doctrine of the ontological Trinity is the Church's attempt to describe the mystery, the mysterious being of God in the light of His self-revelation, in the light of His becoming a Father to His people, of His sending His Son to be their Redeemer, and in the light of His pouring out His Spirit at Pentecost. God, as noted, is not different within Himself than what He presents in the created order. He is Trinity within Himself and yet one God.

Many have sought to deal with the "vestiges of the Trinity" within the created order by seeing patterns of three-ness throughout it. One such pattern is that of steam, water, and ice and how it can be turned from one state to another while remaining one substance (another is gas, liquid, and solid). Both illustrations, although helpful and even sensible, lean towards an error or ancient heresy of the early Church called Sabellianism which suggested that God is one with three aspects or roles (like costumes, if you will, he appears as the Son but is not the Son in his nature only in his role). Other attempts to make the Trinity understandable include the tripartite nature of humanity — spirit, soul, and body, although theologians have contended that humanity is simply spirit/soul and body or dichotomy — as another example of God's three-ness stamped within creation. Illustrations have even found expression on the practical level as many offered a picture of the Trinity as that of a man (one), who is a father, husband, and a son, while still remaining a man (nature). As logical as such sounds, it again brings the doctrine of Trinity to a level of comprehension that removes the fullness of God's nature or three-persons by falling to one polarity or the other. In other words, you either have a substance that has three parts (e.g. steam, water, and ice, none of which can be all three at the same time) or a person that has three roles (husband, father, and son) or just three gods (Tri-theism, which explains the personal interaction among the members of the Trinity, but loses the oneness aspect).

God is not a divided being of three equal parts nor are the personal activities or distinctions something that is added to his nature.

Every analogy has its shortcomings when it comes to explaining God or the Trinity. It is difficult from the created order to provide an illustration of Trinity without lapsing into a heretical notion. If God is beyond our comprehension, then to logically build an illustration that explains Him fully is to reduce Him to our understanding. It is better left a mystery. This is not to say we cannot speak about God or even attempt to explain Him, but only to assert the need to be careful, allowing the awe and mystery of His nature to remain as something we worship.

All of this to say that the ontological essence of God is one. Who He is within Himself is who He is when He presents Himself to us.

Economic distinctions: Economy does not refer to monetary matters, but to the ordering of activities or different functions or activities. That is, the distinct and different roles assumed by the members of the Godhead in the economy of creation and redemption (first taught by Hippolytus and Tertullian). More simply, this is how God relates to the world and to each other for all eternity.

To help us clarify, let's take a look at redemption and how God as Trinity brought it about. In the loving work of redemption, God the Father planned the redeeming process and sent His Son into the world (John 3:16; Galatians 4:4; Ephesians 1:9-10). The Son obeyed the Father and accomplished redemption for us (John 6:38; Hebrews 10:5-7). God the Father did not come and die for our sins, nor did God the Holy Spirit. That was a particular work of the Son. After Jesus ascended back into heaven, the Holy Spirit was sent by the Father and the Son to apply redemption to us. Jesus speaks of "the Holy Spirit, whom the Father will send in my name" (John 14:26), but also says that

He Himself will send the Holy Spirit (John 15:26). The Holy Spirit's role is then to regenerate fallen humanity or give us new spiritual life (John 3:5-8), to sanctify us (Romans 8:13; 15:16; I Peter 1:2), and to empower us for service (Acts 1:8; I Corinthians 12:7-11). One could say generally, that the work of the Holy Spirit seems to bring to completion the work that has been planned by God the Father and undertaken by God the Son.

There was little attempt in the early church to understand the relations among the three (the ontological state or how God exists in Himself as Father, Son, and Holy Spirit); rather, there was a concentration on the ways in which the Triad was manifested in creation and redemption. Triad was first used by Theophilus (2nd century apologist) as he equated the three days of creation, which preceded the creation of the sun and moon, as "types of the Triad, that is, of God and of His Word and of His Wisdom." The economic Trinity is the same Trinity as the ontological. We are simply moving, then, in the order of dogmatic theology from a discussion of God as He is in Himself, a fellowship of Father, Son and Holy Spirit, to discuss how this God reveals Himself in the various roles assumed by the first, the second, and the third persons of the Godhead insofar as God is our redeemer.

Subordination in the economic Trinity: Just when we think we might be headed somewhere in the field of understanding, we come to another mine-field of potential catastrophe. We have thus far argued that the Trinity is equal ontologically, one, and yet three persons with varying roles in the economy of redemption. Scripture seems to imply there is an order or subordination within the Trinity, at least when you are dealing with the economic aspect of the Trinity.

When we speak about subordination within the Trinity we are dealing with the roles or the economy of redemption and not within the ontological reality of the Trinity. Such texts as, "the Father is greater than I," (John 14:28) do indicate subordination is taking place within the Godhead. Although He is eternally the Son and equal with the Father, He is subordinate to the Father as the Messiah. In this way, He becomes the Anointed One and voluntarily submits Himself to the Father in all things, emptying Himself and becoming obedient to the point of death. I Corinthians 15:27ff seems to indicate that the Son shall be subject to the Father forever.

Hippolytus (170-236 a.c.e) affirmed the oneness of God without hesita-tion. However, he affirmed this oneness of God in the three-foldness of His economy. God is not lonely in Himself. God made His Word come forth as an instrument of creation, thus, begotten in this sense, yet eternal. The Word is not an emanation, but is the Son proleptically. Hippolytus does not like the language of eternal Word. The Word is called the Son because He would become incarnate. The early church fathers wrestled with the language of begotten and labored to philosophize the Son as "eternally begotten." The scope of such a discussion is far beyond our purpose. Suffice it to say that Hippolytus affirmed God's oneness in His three-foldness.

Tertullian (160-225 a.c.e.) taught that there were three manifestations of the one God. Although they are numerically distinct or distributions (not division), so that they can be counted, they are manifestations of a single indivisible power. To highlight his emphasis on unity, he illustrates it by pointing to the unity between a root and its shoot, a source and its rivers, the sun and its light. The Father, Son, and Spirit are one identical substance; this substance has been extended into three manifestations. He was the first to talk of "persons" and "substance," and yet did so by trying to keep the unity of the rule. Rule is still substance. One divine substance which is possessed by two persons, in fact by three. He doesn't tell us what person or substance means when applied to the Godhead.

The Old Testament anticipates these roles as the Father is depicted in Malachi 1:6; the Son in Isaiah 53; and the Spirit comes upon men and women (Isaiah 61; Joel 2; Acts 2) — to disclose His will to His people and empower them so that they might fulfill the task which God has for them.

The mistake we make regarding subordination is to assume that priority necessitates superiority. The functions of the Godhead reflect the order of operation that allows for the purpose of creation and redemption to be worked out. For example, a pastor is not greater than a parishioner or a husband greater than his wife. The order, having someone be first, does not require that worth, value, or superiority be placed upon the person. In the same way, the subordination within the Godhead is simply a description of how the Godhead relates to each other as they carry out their roles and offices within the created order and redemption. All of that to say, there is only a subordination of order, office, and function and not a subordination of essence or being.

What is clear about our discussion is that the Bible requires that we affirm the following three statements when it comes to the doctrine of the Trinity.

God is one.

Each person is fully God.

God is three persons.

All heresies distort one or more of these affirmations.

Ancient Heresies: Dynamic Monarchianism, Modalistic Monarchianism, and Arianism.

It would be appropriate to take a moment to highlight some of the major heresies regarding the Trinity. This might help us see the boundaries more clearly that the early church set for us when discussing the triune nature of God. Each of these heresies protect the unity of the Godhead at the expense of the three persons either by reducing them to roles or by reducing Jesus to only a man and making the logos the power that was eternal that was placed within the human Jesus.

Dynamic Monarchianism: This heresy centered around Jesus and the Christ. In essence, God, the monarch, dynamically worked out His will in the man Jesus. This heresy is more aptly called "adoptionism," because God adopted Jesus into the role of Christ due to his virtuous life. Jesus was then a "mere man" upon whom God's spirit descended. The originator of this teaching is Theodotus, a Byzantine leather merchant, in 190 A.D., who denied Christ under a threat of persecution. He felt he did not deny God, just the human Jesus. Malicious critics, however, postulated that his makeshift position was to cover up his apostate act. In any regard, Theodotus believed that prior to baptism, Jesus was just an ordinary man, although, completely virtuous. At the baptism, the Spirit, or Christ, descended upon Him, and from that time He performed miraculous works.

Paul of Samosata, perhaps the most interesting proponent of this type of teaching, found a favorable response in the second half of the third century (condemned at the Third Council of Antioch in 268 a.c.e.). Jesus was not the Word, because the Word (Logos) was not a personal entity. Rather, the term refers to God's commandment or ordinance. God ordered what He commanded in the man Jesus. That is the meaning of "Logos." In this sense, God was radically present in the life of the man Jesus. There was a working or force in the man Jesus that enabled Him to do powerful things, but there was no real substance or presence of God within Him. The appeal of this heresy was minimal.

Modalistic Monarchianism: God, the monarch, works out His will in three modes: Father, Son, and Spirit. In other words, God is not the Father, the Son, or the Spirit, but simply appears in those modes of operation. Modalism seems to affirm the doctrine of Trinity, while Dynamic

Monarchianism denies it. Both heresies attempted to preserve the unity of
God. Modalism was strongly committed to the full deity of Jesus. Since the
Father was the term used to signify the Godhead itself, any suggestion that
the Word or Son was somehow other than the Father upset the modalists. To
them, it seemed you were arguing for bitheism (two Gods). Among those
who embraced this were Noetus of Smyrna (180-200 a.c.e.), Praxeas (180,
brought it to Rome from Africa according to Tertullian), and Sabellius, who
developed the most complete doctrinal conception of this position.

Sabellius: There is one Godhead with three aspects or roles called
Father, Son, and Spirit. These are not real distinctions, but merely names
which are appropriate and applicable at different times. Each role is the same
person or successive revelations of the same person. We have one person
with three different names, roles, or activities.

Arianism: Arius, an incredibly pious and rigorous individual, embraced
the teaching of Lucian of Antioch, who taught the Logos in Christ was just a
power. The fundamental premise of his system was the absolute uniqueness
and transcendence of God, unoriginate source of all reality. He sent to
Bishop Alexander an uncompromising statement which read:

"We acknowledge one God, Who is alone ungenerate, alone eternal,
alone without beginning, alone true, alone possessing immortality, alone wise,
alone good, alone sovereign, alone judge of all, etc."

In this view, since God is unique, transcendent, and indivisible, the being
or essence of the Godhead cannot be shared or communicated. Whatever
else exists must have come into existence, which would mean for Arius that
Christ was created. The error of this view centers on the Son being created
and not an emanation from, or a consubstantial portion of the Father. The
Son is a perfect creature, which created the cosmos because the contingent
world could not bear the Father's direct impact. The Son is distinct from the
rest of creation, but created as Colossians 1:15 and John 1:1 suggest
according to Arius. Jesus is then a pre-existing supernatural being, the
eternal Logos who came into this world and was born and lived as the man
Jesus of Nazareth. Arius contended that although the man Jesus is the
supernatural, pre-existing Logos, highly exalted above all other creatures,
worthy of our reverence, therefore, and our worship, He is not God Himself.
Arius insisted quite strongly on this point. Jesus is subordinate to God and
like us, a creature. According to this heresy, there was a time when Jesus did
not exist. The mystery of the Trinity when explained to human satisfaction —

that is removing the mystery — as was the case in our history and with Arius, inevitably results in a heresy or misrepresentation of the person of God as He is.

We have reviewed these here to give us context for asking the right questions that lead us to right doctrine — and a right understanding of our God, the divine "Us" that has created us with the same DNA ("in His image") that comprise the Trinity. God exists as one and yet three persons, relating to each other, loving each other, and extending that love to the created order. The simplicity of the First and Second Commandments along with the Great Commission of Matthew 28 provides a sense of God's nature and heart. In a nutshell, the Christian life centers itself upon love, and the simplicity of loving God and others. Everything we are called to do in the confines of our churches must embrace this aspect of relationship with God and others. It is the basis by which the divine "Us" exists and operates. If the Church is to resemble its heavenly Father, then we must return to the land of community where oneness and diversity exist side by side; where equality is the basis of every human interaction; where order and function find their place as individuals submit to one another and the various roles provided by God that gives life, order, and health to the relational fabric of our lives, homes, and church communities. If God is an "Us", then we must be an "us" as well.

If life is primarily about relationship then the first relationship that matters most is our relationship with God, loving Him with everything we have (Mark 12:30). It is from this right relationship with God that we find wholeness and fullness in ourselves, having our sense of self and identity properly restored to us, awakened from the slumber of psychological dismay, confusion, insecurity, and lost purpose. The love of God then transforms who we are, from the beast of our fallen sinful state into the princes and princesses we were created to be.

The second relationship that God longs to restore is then with others, loving others as ourselves (Mark 12:31). Jesus made it ever so clear that it is love that marks us as His disciples (John 13:34-35) and the apostle John that boldly asserted that unless we love our brothers we, in essence, do not love God (I John 4:7-11).

As love flows from a harmonious relationship we now have with God and ourselves, we are better able to give away the love that is within (I John 4:19), comforting others with the comfort we have received (2 Corinthians 1:4). It is within this context that we believe the great commission is given as we are commanded by Jesus to make disciples from the vantage point of community.

———

CHAPTER 3

"GOD IS LOVE"

———

What does all this mean for us? How does this affect our understanding of Church? How do we relate to one another based on God as tri-unity? These questions may seem rather rudimentary but somehow the answers have been misunderstood or misapplied in our faith context. After all, as a Church in America or the world for that matter, we are not unified as a whole, living out as one body serving together for the glory of our God. Although we are all saved by the same Jesus and serve the same God, our doctrines and practices divide us to the point that commonality is hard to find. However, the Trinity is centered on one purpose. Each member is given fully to it and each fulfils their role in the order of creation and redemption to facilitate the will and glory of God. Unity for many simply means sameness. The popular language of our culture is diversity and yet sameness is the predominant reality for many churches.

For example, we speak about diversity but we quietly (some not so quietly) detest it. There is that sense of discomfort within when we encounter someone that is different in race, culture, belief, etc. It's almost as if a whisper of disdain is heard within the chambers of the soul as it quietly says, "I can't believe they think (or do) that." As much as we want to say we value others we tend to value sameness (as boring as that might be, it is predictable). The homogenous church is not a picture of heaven but of earth dwellers who find it hard to relate to those that are different. Loving those like you, as worthy as it is, is not an award-winning activity. Jesus made it clear that even the Pharisees greet those that greet them. Or as Dallas Willard boldly asserts, the Mafia is nice to those that are nice to them. Loving those who are not like you and even those who abuse you and use you (Matthew 5:48) requires a super-natural Jesus-like love. This kind of love can only come from the person of the Holy Spirit in yielded hearts that long to reflect the truth and grace of God and exists between the persons of the Trinity. Maybe this has something to do with why the Church in America is so impotent to change our cities and communities.

The love we employ is natural and centered more on the self than upon God, geared more towards personal fulfillment than the extension of God's Kingdom, and tends to decline when not received, rewarded, or acknowledged. In this respect we are much like the world in our practices and lifestyles. That is, those who have a sense of morality in the world.

The difference between a moral pagan (a non-Christian) and a practicing Christian is often very little. The moral non-Christian gives to charities, volunteers some of his time to benefit others, and attends various meetings or societies on a regular basis. The Christian gives to their church, volunteers his time to serve in the church and para-church ministries, and attends church regularly. It's hard to see the difference and many of our research studies (e.g. Barna Research Group) indicate that the behaviors of many Christians are not much different from those who make no profession of faith in Christ.

If we are going to reflect the nature and character of God then we must be a people that live in submission to Him, live in unity with each other as the body of Christ, relationally loving and caring for each other, and enjoying the diversity that so beautifully makes up the mosaic we call humanity. If this is going to happen, and we know it will take the move of God to do so, then we must all be willing to forego our pride and release our fleshly grip on what we believe belongs to us, our lives. Paul makes it clear that we are not our own but have been bought with a price. Like the hand or the foot to our bodies, we are now a part of the Body of Christ. We exist for God's pleasure and His purpose. It is only when we discover this that our lives become complete, whole, and meaningful. As pastors and leaders of our churches, we must release our hold on our ministries. We need to get over ourselves and come back to a place of realizing we are simply servants or stewards of our master's affairs. What we do is about Him. We are servants doing a servant's task. And as Jesus said, no one thanks the servant for doing what he is supposed to do. No matter how big or how small one's church is we are nothing more than servants doing our Father's business.

Scripture also makes it clear that God is love. The Trinity existed eternally in love. That is, the Father loved the Son and the Son loved the Holy Spirit — each loving the other. Our great Church father, Augustine, provided a wonderful description of this love as he said the bond of love that holds the Father and Son together is the Holy Spirit. His analogy was not meant to be a theological description but a relational picture of how God loves. A sense of delight surrounds the Trinity as each member is lovingly engaged to the other and has been doing such before time began.

Philosophically, it is important to note that God is unchanging. Although there has been some dialogue even in conservative evangelical circles that God does change, it is beyond the scope of our discussion here. For our purposes it is essential to note that God must be love within Himself (ontologically), loving eternally. If God became love at creation or is not love within Himself, but becomes love at creation or chooses to demonstrate love as a part of the created order, then we have a fundamental shift in God's nature and person. Who we encounter is then not who He is. He becomes love for the created order but is not within Himself. If this were the case, then God would change fundamentally in creation and would be utterly different in His nature than He is in His expression. God, therefore, must be understood to be loving in eternity and finds a creative expression of that love in the creation of humankind. The loving care He provides the universe is an extension of His very nature and being. "God is love," the apostle writes, and is so from an eternal vantage point. The practical outworking of this key point is that God expresses Himself in creation by loving what He makes and taking great joy in it.

God's love was most clearly expressed when He created Adam and Eve in a moment of creative genius. The pleasure of God in creating Adam and Eve is noted in the early chapters of Genesis as God is so very pleased in what He has made. He is delighted with His offspring as any parent would be. It's like the overwhelming delight of the father who recognizes himself in his newborn son or the mother who sees her eyes in her baby. God made us in His image. Our first parents perfectly reflected that godly image and God was deeply moved. As we shall show in the next chapter, God made us like Himself (not independent beings, God is the "I Am", we are at best, "I am too."). There is no greater gift God could give than to give Himself in creation and He does so by providing Adam and Eve with His image. It is the reflection of Himself in them that brings Him such delight as it would any loving parent (Genesis 1:31).

Let us take a minute to summarize what we have said thus far. The first is that God is one God, not three gods. And yet, the deity of each of the three persons of the Trinity must be affirmed. The second is the threeness and oneness of God is not in the same respect.

We must be careful to stress that God is one and yet three. What we have here is a paradox or mystery. We have argued that the Trinity is incomprehensible by our finite minds, not irrational. In the history of the Church it is important to note that the church councils only provided us with a language to speak properly about God, a fence, if you will. They marked out the boundaries. The doctrine of the Trinity is not an effort to resolve all questions and to make plain all mystery. The function of the doctrine is simply to reflect as accurately as we can the data of Scripture as a whole, thus to preserve the Church from error and find ourselves in a deeper and more reflective relationship with our Creator.

The next aspect concerns the Trinity as eternal. There have always been three: Father, Son, and Holy Spirit. Each is eternal and did not come into existence at some point in time. The fourth is the function of one member, within the economy of redemption that is subordinate to one or both of the members, but does not imply inferiority in being or essence (ontology). Remember, within the ontological aspect the Trinity is not subordinate. The fifth is essential for our understanding of ecclesiology. The Trinity is relational. The Trinity exists in an eternal relationship with one another. It is from this existence, a community of three persons, which comes the relational bent of our God. He is love and maintains relationship with Himself. In some sense a relationship of Father and Son and Spirit in the God-head is analogous to the "I-Thou" fellowship which prevails at the human level when two persons are aware of each other as I and Thou. This is significant, because if God is not personal within Himself then what He presents to us in the created order is not who He truly is within Himself.

If we are correct in our assumption that God's love is eternal — not created for us but given to us because of who He is — then it is imperative for the Church to understand that love is a dominant reality of our existence and practice. After all, Jesus did say that the world will know that we are His disciples because of our love for each other (John 13:34). The application of our church practices and worship services that find themselves devoid of love are nothing more than a loud, irritating gong to God and beautifully scripted pictures of food to a hungry and dying world.

The tragic reality for many is that their experience of God has been a rather bland form of Christianity that has fallen prey to personal interpretation that has forgotten the one thing that makes us Christian: LOVE. As we have already noted, Jesus made it quite clear in the new commandment to His disciples:

Love each other. Just as I have loved you, you should love each other. Your love for one another will prove to the world that you are my disciples. (John 13:34-35)

The defining mark for Christians is that we love God and what He loves — people.

The apostle John makes it clear that God is love. The apostle writes:

Dear friends, let us continue to love one another, for love comes from God. Anyone who loves is born of God and knows God. But anyone who does not love does not know God — for God is love. God showed how much he loved us by sending his only Son into the world so that we might have eternal life through him. This is real love. It is not that we loved God, but that he loved us and sent his Son as a sacrifice to take away our sins. Dear friends, since God loved us that much, we surely ought to love each other. No one has ever seen God. But if we love each other, God lives in us, and his love has been brought to full expression through us.

We know how much God loves us, and we have put our trust in him. God is love, and all who live in love live in God, and God lives in them. (I John 4:7-12, 16, NLT)

It is apparent that the best proof of our love for God is our love for each other. As we love God we find ourselves loving what He loves. For so many in the Western world we have romanticized love to the point that we really don't understand what it means. According to Hollywood, love is that emotional upheaval that takes place when you encounter something so terrific that your heart explodes in ecstatic joy. "If we don't feel it then we can't love" or "we can only love something when we feel it." Now don't get us wrong, feelings are a dynamic aspect to romantic love or any love for that matter. When you love something deeply, your heart is given and, naturally, feelings for the person are there. The point is that love is not about feelings but about an act of the will that engages the heart. Love is an active word that is visible for all to see. To help us here we turn to the work of Christian A. Schwarz, *The 3 Colors of Love*, which describes the fullness of love for us and helps us understand just how much of a relational God we serve. Love is then an act that is relational in nature, involving the heart in activity that seeks to bring justice, truth, and grace for another.

Love is about JUSTICE, which is most clearly expressed by compassion. When we refer to justice here, we are not simply talking about the objective fairness often associated with a court of law or simply making things right in our society. Rather it involves a genuine **compassion** for others that goes beyond legal justice.

Love is about TRUTH, which finds it's greatest expression in being trustworthy. That is God's trustworthy love in action, which means you can trust Him because He is trustworthy and therefore true. Not all things that are true are trustworthy. For example, it is true that Satan is a liar, which does not make him trustworthy.

Love is about GRACE, which is God's accepting love in action. It is hard to give grace if you have not experienced it. Grace is based on a relationship of **acceptance**. It is more than forgiveness. According to the Scripture, it literally means "giving yourself."

To do what Schwarz is calling love requires heart engagement. That is, one cannot love without giving the self in justice, truth, and grace. In other words, love is not love unless you have given yourself. When God loved us He gave us His Son who gave Himself on a cross. The late scholar, Dr. William L. Lane once said, "When God gives a gift, He wraps it in a person." God wrapped His gift in "swaddling cloths" (Luke 2:12) as He gave his Son (John 3:16). Jesus came and gave His life (Mark 10:45) and then sent us the Holy Spirit who gives Himself to regenerating fallen humanity by giving new spiritual life (John 3:5-8), guiding us into all truth (John 16:5-15), empowering us for witness (Acts 1:8), and sanctifying us (Romans 8:13; 15:16; I Peter 1:2).

In our world of overcommitment, stress and deadlines, it is easy to come up with strategies to love that do not involve or even engage the heart. The life of Mother Teresa fully embraced the principle of incarnation. She was often invited by wealthy organizations to speak and share about her ministry. Every non-profit leader is tempted to look at those opportunities as potential gold mines and sharing your vision and need for money is an appropriate and acceptable endeavor in such situations. However, Mother Teresa's message was, **"We don't need your money, we need your time. We want you to give yourself to the poor."** Now keep in mind that there is nothing wrong with giving money to help those in need, but everything wrong with a love that does not engage our hearts, our lives, and our actions.

The true purpose of giving a gift is that when we give it we give part of ourselves with it. And so it is with God, the greatest giver of them all. As He gifted us with the special person of Jesus, He continues to gift us with special people. What a wonderful definition of discipleship — helping others unwrap Jesus.

What we have insisted upon up to this point is that the God we serve is one God who exists or subsists in three persons. This God lives as a community, the divine "Us," if you will. The nature of our God is love and is the motivation behind creation and the redemption of our fallen world. If this is so, then the DNA that makes up the church is also comprised of these elements. We are created to be one and diverse, made for relationship, and motivated by love because we have been loved. We have been made to be a community. We will continue to explore this more in Parts II & III.

PART 2

Ourselves

CHAPTER FOUR

"THE CREATION OF HUMANKIND"

The ancient pages of Genesis make it ever so clear that God's design in creation was centered upon a loving relationship between Him and His creation. The creative genius of God was active in the first six days, culminating in His masterpiece, humankind. God gives the first pair the privilege of intimate relationship with Him, no barrier of sin or shame, the joy of loving each other ("Be fruitful"), and exercising dominion over the land. We must note this is a dominion that works with creation and not against it or to take from it for one's personal gain. The animals lived in harmony with Adam and Eve as did all of the created order. In a sense, we are created to be like God, only dependent upon Him for everything, living out our lives in relationship with Him, with each other, and taking care of the world He has made for His and our pleasure. Our purpose and ultimate fulfillment can only be realized in interdependent relationships — with God and others.

The Creation of Humanity: Genesis 1:27 seems to teach that the Image of God in man is a reflection of the Trinity. Let me illustrate from the ancient pages of Genesis:

A. God created
B. Man
C. In His Image

C. Then in the Image of God

B. He created

A. Him

C. Male and female

B. He created

A. Them.

Creation begins with, and flows from, community. God creates two and places His Image on both. If you'll follow Genesis 1:27, the first line "c" makes it clear that "In His Image" is "man." The second line "c" indicates "the Image of God" is still man, "him." However the third line "c" provides the interpretive key to "man" and "him." That is "Male and Female He created them." The singular "him" moves to a plural "them" in the last line, indicating that the "Image of God" involves both the man and the woman. There is then something about the "Image of God" that involves both male and female. This is not to suggest that marriage is required by the creation account, but to assert, the importance of male and female within the "Image of God" and the reality of community and relationship that is foundational to our existence. It is also of interest to note how polarity is grafted into the original design of creation that makes it clear that unity and diversity are a part of the created order.

Genesis goes on to explain that it was God who spoke in the idyllic garden that "it was not good for man to be alone" (Genesis 2:18, New Living Translation). In other words, built into the fabric of human nature is a relational thread. God did not want us to miss the importance of relationship and so Genesis 2 makes it clear that the human desire for relationship is God-given. The problem is not that we desire relationship, but that we have a "disordered love" (Augustine). That is, we are built to love the Creator first, then the creature, and creation. Our problem often stems from the unfortunate reality that we love the creature or creation first, a "disordered love."

However you slice it, we were not built to be alone. Before we go on, it might be helpful to define what we mean by community. According to Paul D. Hanson, "The community of faith in the Bible is the people called. It is the people called forth from diverse sorts of bondage to freedom, called to a sense of identity founded on a common bond with the God of righteousness and compassion, and called to the twin vocations of worship and participation in the creative, redemptive purpose that unifies all history and is directed to the restoration of the whole creation with a universal order of shalom." (*The*

People Called, Harper & Row Publishers, San Francisco, 1986, p. 467) Community then is God's people sharing life together in Christ. (We will develop this more fully as we go.) The Body of Christ, the Church, provides the greatest place for relationship and community to take place. And yet, what so often comes off as community in our modern era is really nothing more than arranged or strategic relationships that serve the self more than the Body of Christ.

An example of this would be our small group structures. For many churches, our small groups are designed to meet the relational and spiritual needs of our people. This is good and right. Many then join a small group for personal reasons of growth. Again, this is good. The therapeutic elements of our small group benefit many as they learn together, share, and pray for each other. But what so often is the case in our small group structures is that people go for individual reasons that seldom translate into communal realities. Simply, "as long as my needs are being met, then the group is worth the sacrifice of my time." Star Trek's Mr. Spock challenges this notion, (that's right, Spock) as he so powerfully said after his heroic effort of saving the ship at the expense of his life (in the movie, Star Trek: The Wrath of Kahn):

"The needs of the many outweigh the needs of the few, or the one."

The apostle Paul says it this way:

Just as our bodies have many parts and each part has a special function, so it is with Christ's body. We are all parts of his one body, and each of us has different work to do. And since we are all one body in Christ, we belong to each other, and each of us needs all the others. (Romans 12:4-5)

The parts do not determine what the body does, but the head does and that is Christ.

We live in a world where koinonia or fellowship is a commodity that is in high demand but in short supply. No wonder the sitcom *Friends* was such a hit for 10 years as we enjoyed the relationships of six individuals that somehow in spite of encountering great difficulties not only maintained their friendships in the series but more amazingly in real life. This friendship was powerfully forged when the actors decided to band together and negotiate their salaries evenly. Whatever one gets paid, they all get paid — they did not like the idea of one being paid more or less than another. The show involved all six actors and all six should get the same paycheck. Now that is a friend, a team, and reflects rather powerfully the biblical definition of koinonia. God help us find this type of koinonia in our churches!

Hollywood hit another koinonia homerun as they powerfully illustrated what a fellowship or koinonia is in the movie, *The Lord of the Rings: The Fellowship of the Ring*. What Tolkien's world tells us is that fellowship finds it origins in the context of mission. Where there is a purpose greater than ourselves or even the meeting of our own personal needs. Like the nine men in the movie who volunteered for the dangerous mission of returning the ring to Mt. Doom, we find ourselves in a similar situation in our churches and in our world. There is an evasive evil in our world that seeks to destroy us, and most of those that inhabit earth, including many Christians, who are simply unaware of the danger that looms about us. God has placed it on the hearts of His people to make the journey to Mt. Doom, if you will, with the fellowship (that is, of the "Cross") to destroy the evil influence (I John 3:8b). It is a journey that has unenviable odds, enormous obstacles, and armies that outnumber and outclass us at every angle. It is the battle for our families, our cities, our state, our country, and even our world. Our Mt. Doom, like that of Tolkien's world, seems impenetrable by the likes of us and cannot be done by an army of one.

It is only in the "fellowship of the Cross" that we find the full power necessary to defeat the armies of hell. Scripture makes it clear that the gates of hell cannot prevail against the Church (Matthew 16:18). Jesus never said that it will be one church or a denomination that will be able to resist hell, but the Church, unified in the cause of the Mission. It's that Church that hell cannot stop. Maybe that is why Satan works so hard to help us focus on our petty differences, find reasons to fight and disagree, gossip, take sides, etc. If he can keep the army quarreling amongst itself it will lose its focus and eventually destroy itself.

The biblical concept of koinonia, the basis of community, cannot take place unless there is a sense of commonality of heart and purpose — a mission that unites us. Koinonia for the Western 21st Century Christian has been reduced to potlucks or coffee and doughnuts. You know, "stay after the service and enjoy the fellowship." True fellowship can only take place where people are willing to share their lives as they share their hearts for something bigger than themselves.

This is wonderfully illustrated in Paul's relationship with the church at Philippi. The basis of Paul's thankfulness for the people at Philippi is clearly their active participation with him for the sake of the gospel (Philippians 1:

3-5). The word used for partnership is "koinonia", often understood to mean fellowship. Here, it appears that it is referring to an active involvement that would include financial support.

According to Fredrich Hauck, koinonia (κοινωνια), means "participation, impartation, and fellowship" (*Theological Dictionary of the New Testament*, Vol. III, p. 797-798). Paul makes it clear that our fellowship begins with Jesus, "He is the one who invited you into this wonderful friendship with His Son, Jesus Christ our Lord" (I Corinthians 1:9). Koinonia then begins with Jesus as we enter into communion or a relationship with our risen Lord and from that relationship participate in the greater mission.

Koinonia is distinctively a Pauline word, meaning to have something common — "to give a share." It is of interest, that the idea "to give a share" is rare in secular Greek. It is more common in the New Testament, especially in in Paul's writings. The word carries a wide range of ideas from describing a marital relationship to a contribution or a gift. Here, in Philippians 1:5, it is modified by "in the gospel," suggesting a partnership with an active response. Ralph Martin states: "basically it denotes 'participation in something with someone'; and its meaning that Christians share with one another in a common possession (for example, 'the gospel' in 1:5; 'the Holy Spirit' in 2:1) is far more important than the popular modern idea of a personal association with fellow-Christians as when we use the word of a friendly atmosphere in a public meeting." (Tyndale New Testament Commentaries, *The Epistle of Paul to the Philippians*, Tyndale Press, Grand Rapids, MI, 1980, p 46)

Paul's usual meaning is one of participation in the "objective work" of Christ. Out of this partnership comes a genuine and deep koinonia that knits souls together in a way that normal social gatherings at church cannot. Much like Frodo and the Fellowship of the Ring, genuine fellowship takes place when people are committed to a common purpose. Let's unpack this idea of partnership.

References to partnership:

2 Corinthians 8:4, "**sharing** in the gift for the Christians in Jerusalem." (NLT)

Acts 2:42, "and to **fellowship**," koinonia here does not refer only to the concrete community or society of Christians, but also to the relational harmony established in the life of the community.

Galalatians 2:9, "right hand of **fellowship** that we should go."

"To Give A Share" or "Partnership" the idea underlying fellowship:

Philippians 1:5, 7, "**partakers**," cooperation towards the advancing of the gospel.

Philippians 2:1, "**participation** in the Spirit"

Philippians 3:10, "**share** His sufferings"

Philippians 4:14, "**share** my trouble"

Galalatians 2:9, "they accepted Barnabas and me as their **co-workers**"

The Bible makes it quite clear that the early Church was together physically, emotionally, and spiritually. Acts 1:14 tells us that *"They all met continually for prayer."* Luke tells us that the early church shared all things in common (Acts 2:43-47). In simple language, they lived and shared life together and served the Lord together. Even Peter's inaugural sermon that gave birth to the church was not a solitary act. Luke adds a rather stunning fact that *"Peter stepped forward with the eleven other apostles"* (Acts 2:14). This was not about a hero or some superstar that gave birth to the church, but about 12 men, a "fellowship of the Cross", who had given their lives to the person of Jesus, working together to declare the Name that brings life to all who call upon Him. May God help us in our rediscovery of who we are as individuals and as the church become such a fellowship.

As noted, community begins with a mission or purpose in life that is greater than the self. And yet ironically, community cannot take place unless we discover our sense of self, our personhood. Logically, it is hard to give of yourself if you do not know who you truly are. On the other hand, you cannot truly know who you are unless you are in relationship to another. To help us understand this we borrow from Martin Buber a wonderful construct that will help consider the reality of personhood as it correlates to God as Trinity.

Personhood can only be fully known or comprehended when we are in an "I — Thou" fellowship. In other words, the "I" cannot really know it is an "I" unless a "Thou" is present. Practically, for me to know I am tall, dark, handsome or not, etc., requires the presence of another. I am only dark in contrast to someone who is light. The sense of self, the "I" requires a "thou" for personhood to form. From the life of a child we see this illustrated, as the child is a "we" (connected to mom primarily and dad in its early years) before it is an "I." Our sense of self is then formed in the context of another — a community — a "we."

Taking this one step further, for dependent humanity, the "I" cannot fully know itself unless an ultimate "Thou" is present. Simply said, unless we come to know the One who created us, we ourselves will not be fully known. "I" can only know who I am in relationship with the "Thou" (God) of the universe. As I am in relationship with Him and then His creation, a sense of the "I" is developed in relationship to the "Thou" and the "thou" (another) of the created order or penultimate (that which is contingent upon or derives its life from the "Ultimate").

And so, man cannot know who he truly is, the "I", unless he is in relation to a "Thou." Relationship, primarily with God, is what brings ultimate definition. It is clear then that our sense of identity requires the existence of another by whom one is known. Community is then significant and vital to self-understanding and growth. This is why it is so very important for us to be in fellowship with one another. Christians are like pieces of charcoal. When we are in the fire we heat up, but when we take ourselves out of fellowship there is a tendency to cool down. Spirituality is about right relationship with God and right relationship with others, the two Great Commandments of Jesus.

We have been contending that communion or community exists within the Godhead. If you will, the creation account paints God as "Us" (LXX, the Septuagint uses poisomen), as one having dialogue within Himself. There is a reflective process portrayed in the creation account, which suggests the Godhead to be in conversation with Himself. Hence, God as we know Him, is a God who is in relationship with Himself. The late Swiss theologian, Emil Brunner argued that this relational aspect of God was based in His nature of love. The basis of all Christian life is then founded in the simple reality that God is love.

"God is the One who reveals Himself in Jesus Christ as the God for us. The love of Jesus is the love of God. Thus God is not merely the Loving One in His relation to us, but in Himself He is Love. He is not only loving in relation to the world which He has created; He did not begin to love 'only when there was a world,' but He loves 'from before the foundation of the world,' 'from all eternity'; He 'is Love.' This highest and most daring word of the New Testament, and of human speech as a whole, is only possible if the love of God is really 'before the foundation of the world,' if therefore God is in Himself the One who loves.

" . . . From all Eternity He loves His Son, and therefore through His Son He creates the world.

" . . . If God were not in Himself Love, but only became so through His relation to the world, then only in relation to the world would He be personal; in Himself He would be impersonal." (*The Christian Doctrine of God*, Dogmatics, Vol. 1, Westminster Press, Phila, 1949, pp. 228-229).

His Creation (humankind) is then an expression of His very being; the community of love celebrated within the Godhead would be the basis for the type of community created by Him. Therefore, God who is in relationship with Himself creates a people who are to be in relationship with Him and each other. This is where we see and come to better understand the significance of the two great commands as cited by Jesus (cf. Mark. 12:30-31).

CHAPTER FIVE

"IMAGO DEI: LIKE FATHER, LIKE SON"

As we have seen, we are created in His image. What does it mean to be created in the "Image of God"? God is the "I Am" (the "Ultimate"). He is without beginning or end, not driven by need, but by love. Unlike the rest of the created order, including humanity, we are ever so dependent upon Him. We are the "penultimate" (that which derives its existence from the "Ultimate"), Acts 17:28 states, "For in him we live and move and exist." Once God is placed in the context of a person, there is always a sense of anthropomorphasizing God, placing our humanity on Him. God did not exist in eternity as a lonely being that was seeking to fulfill Himself by creating the human race. There is no sense of God being the "millionaire" that eagerly seeks for His future mate to complete Him. God was and is complete within Himself. Scripture does not suggest in any way that God was longing for something or someone to fulfill Him.

Rather, it seems to suggest rather strongly that the desire of love is to give itself to someone. God provides the greatest gift in creation as He gives to Adam and Eve His image. All of humanity is made in the "Image of God." In that moment of God animating the dust of the earth to create humanity, we find a great demonstration of His love as He gives Himself to us in creation. The joy He has is similar to the joy of a parent (as noted above) looking upon their newborn with delight, the baby reflects back something of the parent ("there is daddy's nose").

The jubilant response of God, "it is very good," when Adam and Eve were created indicates his enormous and overwhelming love He has for the pinnacle of the creative process. His climatic design of loving brilliance was found in a man and a woman that God desired to share Himself with.

Humanity is created in "response-ability." That is, Adam was made to respond to God, as was so powerfully illustrated when his bodily existence was animated by the very breath of God (Genesis 2:7). Adam became a living person, not because he took life by the horns and embraced it, but rather received it. Adam was not a self-made man who was rugged and independent. He was dependent. While having dominion and authority, he recognized clearly his need for God. Rather, Adam and Eve were created to respond to the love and grace of God. It is their response to Him, receiving the life He gave that allowed them to do all that He commanded. It is then when we respond first to Him that we find we have the ability to do all that He asks of us.

The order of the creation account makes it clear that God graces us with life (which has been called the "indicative" in theological circles) and then proceeds to offer the command or instruction (the "imperative"). In other words, God never gives the command (the imperative) unless He gives the life and power to do it (the indicative).

With that said, let's take a moment to reflect on what it means to be created in the Image of God. If Christ has come to restore the broken image within, then we'll need to define what that image might look like. The characteristics we will be referring to are extrapolations from the text and provide a sense of how God may have created Adam and Eve. His original design for us can then be stated as follows.

First, we are created for **communion** with God. God dialogues with man, holds communion with him. Man is created in a state of "response-ability" before his Maker. We are relational beings with a desire to be known and to know. Man is in conversation with God. The very first conversation we see in Genesis 2 is one which God initiates. This is then the sequence, God initiates and man responds; God gives life, man responds by living life in dependence upon his Creator.

As we have already stated, the self can only be fully understood in relationship with another. Community is then significant and vital to self-understanding and growth. This is why it is so very important for us to be in fellowship with one another.

The human "I" is, from the outset, restricted by a concrete "Thou," and only comes to know itself fully as a responsible self when this "Thou" is present. This speaks against the self-sufficiency taught by our world today that embraces autonomous reason, knowing things by and of oneself.

Secondly, we are **dependent** beings. Because man cannot be an "I" except by an encounter with the "Thou" (another person), we see that humanness, life in full, is not available to man unless he is dependent upon God.

The creation accounts paint this quite clearly, particularly in 2:7: "then the Lord God formed man of dust from the ground, and breathed into his nostrils the breath of life; and man became a living being." It is precisely this breath which gave man life and is the very breath that still gives man life. John writes: "all things were made by him, and without him was not anything made that was made." (1:3) Life itself comes from God which thrusts us into the land of dependency. We need God for life. He is the ultimate power source.

Third, we are created to take *dominion*. Man has dominion over the earth and is to exercise this by being fruitful and multiplying, filling the earth, and subduing it. This in no way implies that we can do with the earth what we wish and use its natural resources as we see fit. We are called to steward the world and have been given dominion to do so. The abuses by humanity within the created order of nature, the animal kingdom, etc. do not reflect what we believe God intended when He gave Adam dominion. The discussion is beyond our scope but is worthy of some serious reflection.

Fourth, we possess *mental transcendence*. Not only is man able to rule over the creative order, but he transcends it mentally by being able to reflect upon his experience and order it. We see this clearly demonstrated by the naming and classifying of the animals. Man is able to impose structure upon his existence or experience. In the creative order then, man is not of the same class. His counterpart is not the animals but another human, a "thou." In this case, the "thou" is a female. Although I do not believe that male and female make up the Image of God, I do believe that being in the Image of God involves the only proper counterpart at the horizontal level, the female. The man somehow understands himself better as male in relation to the female, just as the female finds her existence as female in relation to the man. This is not to say that marriage is required by the creation account, but to assert the importance of male and female within the confines of the "I" and "Thou" paradigm proposed earlier. Again, there is a sense of coming to know oneself better as one is in relationship to another.

Fifth, we are created with the power of *volition* and *moral choice*. Adam and Eve understand the difference between right and wrong. This is expressly implied in the passage as God tells the man: "You may eat of every tree in the garden; but of the tree of the knowledge of good and evil you shall not eat, for in the day that you eat of it you shall die." (2:17) So, we know the difference between right and wrong (conscience) and have the ability to choose. There is something innate in all human beings that speaks to the issues of morality.

We are then able to choose God. To be more specific, man is able to respond to God's call by responding to Him in obedience. Hence, man is able to choose God. We are created in response-ability. The power of volition is still with us.

Our fallenness is most readily noticed in our unfortunate ability to refuse to take responsibility for our lives in the truest sense of the word. We do not admit to the real goals of our hearts (Isaiah 50:10-11), which is nothing more than self-protection and self-preservation. As a matter of fact, the "why's" of a person's behavior can best be understood by looking at the direction, or goals they are pursuing. To understand better why we do something, we need to look at the goals we are pursuing (e.g. being happy, feeling good at all times, wealth, etc.). This is assuming that behavior is movement based. Jesus offers some great counsel here in Matthew 6:21: "For where your treasure is, there your heart will be also." If this is the case then we can simply say that volition is tied to the heart. How then do we know what we really treasure? For now, the T.E.R.M. test is probably one of the clearest to discern one's heart. Where we spend our Time, Energy, Reflection, and Money is what has our hearts.

We have been created to be *fruitful*. The process of Kingdom living involves life begetting life. The creative God we serve enjoys His creation multiplying itself. The original command to Adam and Eve included the instruction to "multiply and fill the earth" (Genesis 1:28). The original design of creation has fruitfulness built into it. We are to multiply. The teaching of Jesus regarding the vine and the branches in John 15 makes the point of fruitfulness rather forcefully. Jesus declares, "My true disciples produce much fruit. This brings great glory to my Father." (John 15:8) Christianity is grace-based in every way, but we must not forget that the DNA of our God is in us and if we are plugged into the Vine, then we will portray characteristics that reflect that He is our Father. After all, like Father, like son.

CHAPTER 6

"HOW HUMANKIND COMES TO KNOW GOD"

Jesus answered, "I am the way and the truth and the life. No one comes to the Father except through me." — John 14:6

Truth is a Person. The Way is a Person. Life is a Person.
The Person is Jesus Christ — the only access to the Father.

I am the gate; whoever enters through me will be saved. He will come in and go out, and find pasture. — John 10:9

We are created for communion with Him. We are created in His image. And yet, the gulf of sin breaks the original bond of fellowship we have with our Father. Core to the Christian faith is the person and work of Jesus Christ. Not only is He the restorer of the Image in us, He is also the bridge across the gulf. But how do we really come to know Him in His fullness? Once the Holy Spirit illumines our heart and regeneration takes place, what then? How do we come to know this Person who is the Way, the Truth, and the Life?

How we come to know the Way: Incarnation through His Body

So much of our Christian practice since the Enlightenment has shifted from praxis to discovering truth; that is an acquiring of knowledge for the sake of knowledge. There is something about the gaining of knowledge that smacks of the fallen nature. This is not to suggest that acquiring all knowledge is a bad endeavor, but to assert that there is often more going on. In seeking knowledge, as we so often do, one is attempting to define an item by classifying it and placing it into various classes. In doing so, however, one is inevitably limiting the item and making it finite ("defining" it). The aim of gaining objective information about an item is to basically bring it under one's understanding and control. If our knowledge of God is primarily objective, then our faith process is reversed, as we are doing nothing more than trying to define God and place Him under our control. You can know information about a person, (which is not the same as knowing the person) or you can know the person (which does not negate factual knowledge — it actually enhances it).

The aim of early Christianity was not on learning truth for truth's sake, but applying it to one's life of faith — you know, "walking the talk." William Ames (1576-1633), the Calvinist theologian, captures the heart of what we are trying to say in the very beginning of his book, *The Marrow of Theology*, "Theology is the doctrine or teaching [doctrina] of living to God." (Labyrinth Press, Durham, NC, 1968, p. 77) The aim of any doctrine is to move us to right living ("Clothe yourselves with the armor of right living, as those who live in the light." Romans 13:12, NLT).

As a matter of fact, the division of theology (biblical, practical, dogmatic, etc.) was relatively unknown before the rise of rationalistic philosophy during the Enlightenment era. Before then, the aim and practice of theologians was primarily spiritual. Even when they used scholastic methods, it was to know God more so that one might more completely worship and love him with the fullness of one's heart. One can see such an aim in the work of Anselm (12th century Bishop of Lyon) as he penned his theological work on the existence of God, the *Proslogion*, in the form of a deeply moving prayer. This was not theology simply written to prove God's existence, but a theology that was fully submitted and desired to be more so. One cannot help read such works and not be touched within the confines of one's heart. Mike recalls sitting in a church history class some years ago as one of the students reflected on Anselm's work. He was in awe and was deeply moved as his reflection indicated, "Reading the Anselm made me want to love God more."

Theology was previously known as the "queen of the sciences" not because of its sheer academic prowess, but because it promoted the highest end for humanity: knowing God and possessing life in eternity with God. A purely academic theology would have been foreign to the theologians and pastors of our history. Theologians of old understood theology to be the rational and exact expression of the believer's reflection and experience of God. Due to this belief, theology was then understood to be spiritual. It must be stated that true theology arises from personal experience of God in Jesus Christ, and then reflecting on that experience which leads to a deeper awareness or experiential knowledge of God. One cannot study the glory of God without being affected by that glory (you can't be in the sun for long without your skin changing) — an affect that results in praise and adoration.

Bob Logan has said that in the United States "our knowledge is often beyond our obedience." We know more than we practice and still seek out more knowledge with the hope that this seminar or book will trigger the explosive church growth we are looking for. The bookshelves of countless leaders are lined with notebooks, tapes, and videos of a myriad of seminars and teachings that lie dormant impacting the bookshelf far more than the life of the leader. After all, how much information can one absorb effectively until one actually practices the things one has learned? Maybe we have sought out more information at the expense of the foundational principles of the "Way."

"There must be a way that I can find that will allow my church or ministry to realize its fulfillment in the purposes of God," cries the heart of many faithful servants of God. And yet, for all the "way's" we have created, it is appallingly sad that many leaders are still lost, frustrated, and often find themselves leading in cruise control (this is a passive form of resignation that helps deaden our frustration) or worse, wanting to give up. Finding the "Way" for the 21st Century pastor or leader is often centered upon a new teaching or methodology that has been tested and tried by a gifted and creative leader. Thank God for our gifted pastors, teachers, and leaders who tirelessly seek to find ways to communicate the richness of the Gospel to a world that is not always eager to hear the good news or at least, our presentations of the good news. Unfortunately, our pragmatic thrust in the United States has led to some rather shallow practices that have only focused on the end result. The question of the hour for most practitioners is "does it work?" or "how can this work for me?" Obviously we want things to work, the universe set in motion by our God works and so, is it wrong to ask such questions? Absolutely not!

The problem is not the question but our confusion of trying to find the "Way" in the midst of our religious practices and ecclesiological philosophies. Our post-Enlightenment mind has blinded us from how we come to know the Way. If truth is primarily propositional, then all that is needed is the correct teaching or information, data like a computer program would need. As long as we have the right information then the human program should be able to sort it out and arrange it properly so that the desired outcomes are experienced.

Complicating this quest to know the "Way" in the United States are the central values of our culture. Our world values and places great importance on attractiveness, achievement, and affluence. For many of us, our sense of self depends upon how well we measure up to these identity-conquering values that operate ever so quietly in the psyche of every pastor and leader.

No matter how we slice it, the thrust of our religious, corporate culture is still on "attendance, buildings, and cash." The language of most leaders is opposed to such, but the practice, concerns, and who we celebrate indicate that we have not departed all that far from the culture. Our fight for meaning, value, and self-worth often challenges us to surrender those things that matter most and in so doing, we often lose sight of how we come to know the "Way." Again, maybe some of the foundational principles of the "Way" have been lost. More will be said on this later.

All of that to say it is the reality of a loving and caring God that alleviates and heals the issues of the soul as people discover God in the midst of a community called the Church. Although the Church teaches that God is a person, we often act as if He is a cosmic force or entity that can be manipulated if one follows the Bible, prays regularly, gives to the church, and lives right. In other words, if we live right then God will bless us and cause all to go well in our life, including adding numerical and financial increase to our ministries. For the most part, in the Western world, particularly since the Enlightenment, we have reduced relationship with God to right belief or action – behavioral issues rather than heart issues. Like the Pharisees of old, we have some wonderfully holy people in regard to behavior, but far from holy with regard to heart (see Matthew 7:21-23 and Matthew 23).

All of this leads us to this potent question — How are we to understand the process of coming to know the "Way" (more specifically, revelation)? We know the primary result of revelation is the knowledge of God. By this, we are referring to a knowledge not only of the person of God, but also of what He has done, of His creation, of the nature and situation of man, of the relationship between God and man. For our purposes, we will focus only on how we come to know the "Way." To help us grasp this more fully, let's pause and take a look at faith. Since it requires faith to know the "Way" it might help us here to understand what we often mean by faith and what it actually means to have faith.

Faith As Assent: The Latin word is *assensus*, the closest English word we have to describe this type of faith is assent. This is faith as belief — that is, giving one's mental assent to a proposition, believing that a claim or statement is true (e.g. "The tree is tall"). This is better known as a propositional understanding of faith and is the dominant norm for the church today. Faith as assent is where we get the notion about belief being a "head" matter, which has allowed us to create a false dichotomy between the "head" and the "heart." This is a recent development in the history of the Church and was birthed, primarily, from two developments in modern Western Christianity: The Protestant Reformation and the Enlightenment.

The Protestant Reformation we are referring to is not so much what Martin Luther did (based on a personal encounter with God) but the fallout that took place over the next decades that resulted in a series of protests within the confines of the newly forming Protestant tradition. The Protestant Reformation not only emphasized faith, but also produced a number of new denominations that distinguished themselves by what they believed, e.g., Lutherans believed a, Presbyterians believed b, Baptists believed c, etc. Over time, the Christian faith came to be about believing the right things, having "right" belief instead of "wrong" beliefs. This development changed the meaning of the word "orthodoxy." Before the sixteenth and seventeenth centuries, orthodoxy referred to "right worship" or "correct worship." The gradual emphasis within the church moved toward being right doctrinally without as much, if any, concern at times with being righteous or in right relationship with God.

The second development was the birth of modern science and scientific ways of knowing in the Enlightenment era of the seventeenth century. One of the effects of the Enlightenment is truth was identified with factuality: truth is that which can be verified as factual. The Enlightenment called into question the factuality of parts of the Bible and of many traditional Christian teachings due to the rise of the scientific method. The church at that time was responding with faith declarations within the scientific tradition, resulting in a faith that came to be about what was true, verifiable, and factual only.

Faith As Trust: This is faith that is represented as a radical trust in God as a person and is most clearly what is represented by faith in the Scripture. James makes it clear that faith is not just about right belief as he challenges the believers of his day: "Do you still think it's enough just to believe that there is one God? Well, even the demons believe this, and they tremble in terror! (2:19, NLT). One can believe without submitting the heart or trusting. One can believe something without trust or yielding the heart. And so, faith does not necessarily mean believing all the right things about God or knowing all the right things about God, but about trusting God. If revelation, knowing the "Way," is primarily regarded as the presentation of a person, then faith will correspondingly be viewed as an act of personal trust or commitment to that person. Theology then is not simply a set of doctrines that have been revealed. It is the Church's attempt to express what it has found in God's revelation of himself, based on a personal encounter with the living God. It is only when one has encountered God that one may legitimately speak about what has been encountered and discover the "Way". Theology then grows out of personal relationship or communion with God. That is why it can be said that the opposite of faith as trust is not doubt or disbelief, but mistrust. More specifically, the opposite is "anxiety" or "worry." Jesus instructs us to not worry, in other words, "Don't worry about everyday life" and then adds, "You have so little faith" (Matthew 6:25-33 and Luke 12:22-31). Little faith and anxiety go together. Simply, the person who worries or is anxious is a person who lacks trust in God. We can measure the degree of faith we have by the amount of anxiety in our lives.

Faith As Faithfulness: This is faith that is faithful to God, which means loyalty, allegiance, the commitment of self at its deepest level, the commitment of the heart. This type of faith is not faithfulness to statements about God, but faithfulness to God as revealed in the Incarnation, the Bible, and the life of the believing community. The opposite of faithfulness or fidelity is infidelity, being unfaithful to our relationship with God. To use the biblical metaphor, the opposite of this meaning of faith is adultery. Another biblical term for infidelity is idolatry, which is giving one's ultimate loyalty or allegiance to something other than God. Faith means being loyal to God and not to the many would be gods that present themselves to us. It means loving God and loving our neighbor and being faithful, above all, to these two great relationships. More practically, it means paying attention to our relationship with God, not only "not straying," but being mindful and attentive to the relationship. Much like a marriage, we find our relationship with God grows, like that with our spouses, when we are attentive to the relationship. We are attentive to our relationship with God through worship, prayer and the life of compassion and justice as we reflect the light and love of Jesus. To be faithful to God not only means to love God, but to love what God loves, namely, one's neighbor, and indeed the whole of creation.

Hopefully this detour has helped you realize that the journey we are on is not simply about propositional realities (as necessary as they are), but about an intimate encounter with God that leads to a life of transformed faith and practice. You *discover* the Way when you discover the Person. In other words, you come to know the way as you come to know the person of Jesus. The text in John 14:6 makes it quite clear that Jesus is the Way to God as the passage is set in the context of Jesus explaining to His followers that He must go to the Father (John 14:1-7). In other words, He not only shows us the way (by revealing it), but He is the way (by way of redeeming humanity). The language of the passage makes this ever so clear that Jesus is the Way, "no one can come to the Father except through me" (NLT).

A logical progression could be understood in the Johannine passage, but the natural force of the passage should be taken as "truth" and "life" being governed by the "way." (That is epexegetical or explanatory which means "that is to say", although the three nouns, way, truth, and life, each contain a definite article allowing for the interpretation that the three nouns are co-ordinate.) There is a sense where the definite article with each noun could add an interpretive force of Christ as the real (The Ultimate) way, truth, and life; all other ways, truths, and lives are transitory. For our purposes, we will treat and explicate each (way, truth, and life) as it correlates to the relational and communal reality of our God.

He is the Way because He is the truth — the full revelation of God — and He is the Way because the life of God is in Him (As John makes clear in 1:4, 12-13; 5:26). We then see that Jesus as the "way" depicts Him in His mediatorial role (the bridge, that connects us to the Father) between God and humanity as He paves the way through His death and resurrection to the Father ("The Father's house" John 14:2). Jesus is not presenting Himself primarily here as a moral guide or example for the disciples to follow. Jesus is the gate ("Yes, I am the gate. Those who come in through me will be saved." John 10:9), by which humanity can enter into relationship with God the Father. All this is so, because Jesus is the Truth. Jesus as the "truth" (embodiment of God's self-revelation, Hebrews 1:3) is the mediator of the revelation of God. When Jesus refers to himself as the truth he is not dealing with truth ontologically, but describing himself in terms of his mission to the world. Jesus said. "I was born for that purpose. And I came to bring truth to the world. All who love the truth recognize that what I say is true." (John 18:37) Jesus shows us the Father (John 1:18) and as he, as the truth, mediates the full revelation of God. As the truth, Jesus enables us to know the way, (the goal of going to the Father). The destination of the way is relationship with the Father, going to the Father's house. This life the Father has given to the Son (John 5:26) who alone can give it to those who believe in Him (John 10:28). Jesus as the "life" is then the mediator of the life in God that only comes by way of salvation. Life comes by way of truth. That is, those who believe in Jesus as the incarnate revelation of God receive the gift of life so that the words of Jesus are the source of life (John 5:24; 6:63). Jesus is then true light that gives light to a dark world, revealing the fullness of God as the one and true way to the Father (John 1:4, 9).

Thomas a' Kempis drives our point home for us in his great work, the *Imitation of Christ*.

"Follow thou Me: 'I am the way, the truth and the life.' (John 14:6). Without the Way, there is no going; without the Truth, there is no knowing; without the Life, there is no living. I am the Way, which you ought to follow; the Truth, which you ought to believe; the Life, which you ought to hope for. I am the Way inviolable, the Truth infallible, the Life unending. I am the Way that is straightest, the Truth that is highest, the Life that is truest, the Life blessed the Life uncreated. If you remain My way: 'Ye shall know the truth and the truth shall make you free.' (John 8:31, 32), and you shall lay hold on eternal life." (56.1, Whitaker House, New Kensington, PA, 1981, p. 207)

Jesus is also being portrayed as the norm of life — a picture of what a human being fully submitted to the Father could be. The apostle John understood truth to be a sphere of action, what one lives, as well as what one believes and knows (more on this in the next chapter). Jesus then establishes the norm or standard by which all children of God can live. After all, He came so that He might lavish life upon us (John 10:10).

It is then the Word becoming flesh (Incarnation) that allows us to know who God is. As we noted earlier, the writer of Hebrews says, "But now in these final days, he has spoken to us through his Son. God promised everything to the Son as an inheritance, and through the Son he made the universe and everything in it. The Son reflects God's own glory, and everything about him represents God exactly" (Hebrews 1:2-3; cf. John 5:19-23; 14:9-11). It is through Christ as our sacrifice that we find salvation as "God made Christ, who never sinned, to be the offering for our sin, so that we could be made right with God through Christ" (2 Corinthians 5:21; cf. Romans 5:9-11). This sacrifice, although for all, will not be applied by everyone unless one receives it by faith in Jesus Christ (Romans 4:22-25). We must cross the Bridge (Christ) to access the way to the Father.

This is solid and classic theology that has been passed down since the Apostles. The centrality of the cross and the finished work of Christ are critical to everything we are discussing. Jesus is the Way and is so in every way for the salvation of our souls and the ongoing development of our Christian lives. He not only is the Way, but also lives the way (the norm of life), revealing and modeling for us how a person loves God with His whole heart, loves others as himself, and makes disciples. He is the standard and the goal, not only in regard to salvation (way) and teaching (truth) but showing us how to live (life).

The fruit of the Spirit in Galatians 5:22-23 captures this standard of fullness for us and maybe should be the assessing criterion we use for our individual and corporate lives. It is possible to grow numerically as a church without growing in spiritual maturity. This is not to say that growing numerically or obtaining more biblical knowledge is shallow or wrong as is sometimes indicated by the church purist. Surely we would all love for more to come to know the great truth of Jesus Christ and find salvation and healing in Him. Christian A. Schwarz's work on *Natural Church Development* is a welcome relief as it seeks to aim us towards church health with the presupposition that God has already placed within the church "growth automatisms" (those elements that create growth naturally and "all by itself"). Schwarz does not polarize church health and growth, but rather believes that as congregations "certain developments appear to happen all by themselves, or automatically" (*Natural Church Development*, p. 12). As noted above, truth is a sphere of action, how one lives, not only what one believes and knows.

One comes to know the Way only in that he or she comes to know the Person of Jesus. It is vital to note that Jesus does not say that the truth is discovered first but that one comes to know the Way first. If you'll permit us to draw this out, what Jesus is saying as it pertains to us as the church is that we need an access code, a gate, a door, etc., that allows us entrance to relationship with God. That is, we come to know God personally and intimately through the Incarnation, Jesus pitching His tent among us and living with us. God sent His Son to our broken and sin-filled planet as an act of love and redemption, as well as, an act of war on the spiritual forces that seek to destroy the very creation He so wonderfully made (1 John 3:8b). The very fact that the "Word became human and lived here on earth among us" (John 1:14) is the foundational key to discovering the way. If you want to know the way, then you must follow Jesus as you live out your salvation on a daily basis understanding that the one who loves God also loves his brother (I John 3:15-19; I John 4:7-11).

Let us simplify this for you by mirroring the truth of incarnation, which is another way of saying let's look at the other side of the coin. As Jesus has come and lived His human life (one side of the coin), the truth of this reality is most evidenced when we incarnate the gospel, His presence and His life, "Christ in us" (the other side of the coin). As we receive the incarnation of God, Christ in us, then we live the incarnation before others. The Apostle writes, "He comforts us in all our troubles so that we can comfort others" (2 Corinthians 1:4). The greatest evidence of the incarnation received is when we love others (John 13:34-35), the distinguishing mark that characterizes us as Christ's disciples.

If knowing the Way involves knowing the Person of Jesus, then we must assume that the basis of our interaction with God and His creation is personal and relational. The divine "Us" or Trinity makes a strong case for the relational and communal aspect of our God that is based in His nature of love. This is most clearly portrayed by the followers of Christ loving each other as they live out this Christian faith as a community that is both comprised of the one and the many, unified and yet diverse. The Apostle John provides a strong exhortation here as he writes:

Dear friends, let us continue to love one another, for love comes from God. Anyone who loves is born of God and knows God. But anyone who does not love does not know God—for God is love. God showed how much he loved us by sending his only Son into the world so that we might have eternal life through him. This is real love. It is not that we loved God, but that he loved us and sent his Son as a sacrifice to take away our sins. Dear friends, since God loved us that much, we surely ought to love each other. No one has ever seen God. But if we love each other, God lives in us, and his love has been brought to full expression through us. And God has given us his Spirit as proof that we live in him and he in us. Furthermore, we have seen with our own eyes and now testify that the Father sent his Son to be the Savior of the world. All who proclaim that Jesus is the Son of God have God living in them, and they live in God. We know how much God loves us, and we have put our trust in him. God is love, and all who live in love live in God, and God lives in them. (I John 4:7-16)

Churches might actually find themselves enjoying the fruit of spiritual growth that would add to their number if they returned to the simple world of community. Our churches might actually grow if we were genuine, loving, and faithful believers, committed to the greater purposes of God.

How We Come To Know the Truth: Object or Subject

We have already made some preliminary remarks in the previous chapter about how we come to know the truth. It was made clear (hopefully) that knowing the "Way" is about knowing the Person of Jesus. Jesus, the person, is "the Way, the Truth, and the Life."

Understanding the nature of truth and how it applies to our lives is vital for the growth of the human heart/spirit. We have already touched on how our modernistic world has worked so hard to understand truth that in its study of it, objectified it, and conveniently objectified human nature in the process, reducing humanity to an explanation of biological and electrical impulses and accidence in a random explosion of creation. This has left the human race in a quandary, providing answers for our existence that do not answer the deeper questions of life. Science can often explain the "what" but cannot answer the "why." This is precisely where theology and philosophy come into play. This is our beginning point, understanding that the "why" of life is that which explains the "what" of our existence. Our quest in this book is not to provide you with an argument for the existence of God — we will assume it — nor to provide you with an epistemology for the human race. Our hope is to engage you in a dialogue that will allow those who particularly align themselves with the redeemed in Christ to wrestle with the nature of God, who we are in light of who God is, and the nature of the Church.

This quest we are embarking upon involves a great deal of processing and potentially dismantling some of our theological understanding of God. It would help us here to deal with the dialectical (called "law of polarity" by Christian A. Schwarz) reality of life. That is, for every "thesis" there is an "anti-thesis," and both sit in creative tension with each other. Removing one or emphasizing one over the other cannot resolve them. This creative tension is like the strings of a guitar. Each is necessary for the guitar to make music. The strings, like theology, must be tuned to the proper key. The goal is not sameness for every string but for contrast and tension that provides melodious music when tuned properly.

The method we will rely upon is the dialectical approach that seeks to synthesize between two polarities. By doing so, we will be interested in understanding the issue in full tension that allows for the full expression of a truth.

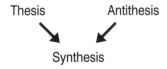

By dialectic, we are not implying that truth is always a mixture of two sets of postulates that sit in diametric opposition, but only affirming the reality that truth is often somewhere in between the extremes, requiring a synthesis that allows for the fullness of the truth to be known.

And so, the opposite poles exist in our experience of life as the delightful tension that enriches our human experience as is so magnificently exhibited by the male and female of our species. You know, the stereotypical descriptions of men: task based, driven by what they see, solution centered, don't feel, etc.; and women: emotional, driven by relational needs, process based, etc. It is this tension that makes for the dynamic we call marriage and the enjoyment (and sometimes confusion) we experience. The polarities provide color to what would be a rather black and white (dull) life. These polarities add spice to a rather bland existence.

We say all of this to suggest that theology, and more specifically our ecclesiology, tends to focus on one polarity at the expense of the other. God is then reduced to a "cosmic principle" or power source on one end or a lonely father who will do anything for relationship with His creation on the other. One camp emphasizes the polarity of God's holiness while the other seeks to make God's love the end all of their focus. Both polarities are necessary and right, but in and of themselves, leave us just shy of knowing the real God as manifested in Jesus Christ.

Christian A. Schwarz has done a masterful job of dealing with the polarities of love in his new book, *The 3 Colors of Love*. He has undergone a personal paradigm shift of his own in his realization that healthy churches are loving churches. He then goes on to deal with the more complete definition of real love. Love is then comprised of justice, truth, and grace.

Love as Justice: Desires to bring deliverance and freedom as it seeks to destroy the oppressive forces and structures that keep people in bondage. That is God's compassionate love in action. This is not simply about the objective fairness often associated with a court of law. Rather it includes a genuine compassion for others that goes beyond legal justice. True justice is expressed in compassion that acts on behalf of the other.

Love as Truth: Challenges and confronts, as it desires the best for the person. That is God's trustworthy love in action. This is more than mere honesty but implies trustworthiness. Love is true and this implies the person doing the loving is true and trustworthy. The Pharisees model for us the opposite of what it means to love in truth. Jesus indicts them, "The teachers of religious law and the Pharisees are the official interpreters of the Scriptures. So practice and obey whatever they say to you, but don't follow their example. For they don't practice what they teach" (Matthew 23:2-3). Being trustworthy is then a person whose private life matches their public life. Love that is true is trustworthy (faithful).

Love as Grace: Accepts and believes in the person. That is God's accepting love in action. Grace is based on a relationship of acceptance. It is more than forgiveness. According to the Scripture, it literally means giving yourself. "And while he was still a long distance away, his father saw him coming. Filled with love and compassion, he ran to his son, embraced him, and kissed him…'We had to celebrate this happy day. For your brother was dead and has come back to life! He was lost, but now he is found!' " (Luke 15:20-32). Love that is gracious accepts people where they are and believes the best about them.

Schwarz is making a case that love is fully love only when all three dimensions of justice, truth, and grace are in place. They each must exist in relationship with the other for the fullness of love to exist. It is easy to focus on one or two of these components, and forget about the others. When that takes place the light and love of Jesus becomes darkened.

The reason our love is incomplete is that it is often centered on the self. We often work out our personal wounds, lack, injury, etc., in the arena of life. All too often what we are doing when we "love" others is nothing more than rubbing salve over our own hurts or absolving or appeasing our conscience. Granted, the actions can be beneficial at times but it is not the love the Bible exhorts us to have. We live in a world full of outrage that often converts its anger into angry plans of attack and destruction. As a matter of fact, a great deal of our social action and political reform is often fueled by anger; the results are nearly always worse than the conditions that provoked the action.

Permit us a rabbit trail here, if you would. We want to jump to some ecclesiological application of this thought. The following is what happens to love when one or two of the aspects are missing. We'll illustrate it for you describing various kinds of churches.

The Grace Church — No Backbone, Non-confrontational: This is a church that focuses only on loving people by acts of mercy like listening, serving the needs of those less fortunate, sympathizing with the wounded and lost, and never correcting those in the throes of sin and despair.

Without truth and justice in operation, "Grace Churches" are prone to the following:

Error: Believing things about God and the Christian life that are not true.

Sinful behavior runs rampant and the reason for this is the belief that love does not confront, but accepts people where they are and so, they do. The problem is that true love will not leave them where they are.

Codependent behavior that allows the hurtful behavior to continue.

Injustice: since they won't do anything to change or help fix the problem, the hurtful actions will continue ironically allowing injustice to flourish.

The Corrective — Tell the truth. Jesus lovingly accepts the woman caught in adultery, but also tells her truth, "Go and sin no more." In other words, don't do that again. "Then Jesus stood up again and said to her, "Where are your accusers? Didn't even one of them condemn you?" "No, Lord," she said. And Jesus said, "Neither do I. *Go and sin no more.*" (John 8: 10-11).

The Truth Church — No Mercy: This is frequently seen in churches or groups that stress both justice and truth, but lack the practical understanding of grace. They might have the "right" topics on the agenda and even do some of the "right" things, but rather than communicating them in a spirit of grace, their fight for biblical goals comes across as hard-hearted, harsh, and intolerant.

Without grace and justice in operation, Truth Churches are prone to the following:

Legalism (Phariseeism): Christianity is rule based, one lives to enforce the law and not break it — Christians consider themselves God's police force, enforcing the law by busting those who break it and giving citations.

Judgmental and not accepting of people, unless others are like what they are like, act as they act and hate what they hate.

Actions are fueled by anger not love. Often create confrontational situations that are sparked by an angry and judgmental spirit.

David and his six hundred men at Ziklag (I Sam 30) illustrate how anger and bitterness often fuels our activities. David and the six hundred men were off on a military mission with King Achish of Gath and had left their wives and children at Ziklag unprotected. A raiding band of Amalekites, longtime enemies of Israel, came down on the village, captured the women and children for slaves, looted the place, and carried off all that mattered, leaving behind nothing but smoking rubble. When David's men returned they were not greeted by a warm smile or "Daddy, you're home," but by smoldering rubble. The six hundred men were a volcano of lament that soon turned into anger, a great anger against David. The text tells us "When David and his men saw the ruins and realized what had happened to their families, they wept until they could weep no more. David's two wives, Ahinoam of Jezreel and Abigail, the widow of Nabal of Carmel, were among those captured. David was now in serious trouble because his men were very bitter about losing their wives and children, and they began to talk of stoning him. "But David found strength in the Lord his God" (I Samuel 30:3-6). If we are going to do something about what's wrong with the world — that's everything from marital fights to world wars, from disobedient children to saving the whales — we have to acquire a better base to work from than anger.

The story continues with David and his men as they find the Amalekite encampment, kill the Amalekites, and retrieve their families and stolen items. In the midst of the victory, some of David's men were angry with the two hundred men that did not go with them because of being too tired. They said, "They didn't go with us, so they can't have any of the plunder. Give them their wives and children, and tell them to be gone" (I Sam 30:22).

Without grace and justice, what often transpires is fueled in self-centered anger that has no mercy or understanding. It can appear as justice, but it is centered in personal anger and often personal injustice that has been experienced by the individual.

The Corrective — Be Merciful and Think of Others — Being about truth, trustworthy, is not about being right and correcting every wrong, but about setting things right: David provides the corrective for us in that he acts in mercy and justice, exhorting his men "No, my brothers! Don't be selfish with what the Lord has given us. He has kept us safe and helped us defeat the enemy. Do you think anyone will listen to you when you talk like this? We share and share alike—those who go to battle and those who guard the equipment"(I Samuel 30:23-24).

David's men are technically right, the two hundred men did not go and in that sense, don't deserve the spoils. However, there is a higher truth here that David works with that involves the reality of family that is founded in grace and justice.

There is a time for a police officer to enforce the law, but not when the building is burning down and people are at risk of losing their lives. This is not the time to write the citation and correct the person; it is the time to save lives.

The Justice Church: This is the church that is all about being fair. It is the church that is upset with the pain, suffering, homelessness, and every injustice in our world and seeks to change it. On the flip side, those who stress truth and grace without justice place their focus on doing the right thing, which often falls short of challenging and seeking to change the oppressive structures. Charity is about helping the victims. Justice asks, "Why are there so many victims?" and then seeks to change the causes of victimization.

Without truth and grace in operation, Justice Churches are prone to the following:

Allows anger and personal agendas to dominate as long as oppressive systems are being destroyed. Never mind the irony that while one oppressive system is being annihilated another is being created.

Reduces the gospel to social action only, providing release with very little, if any, content (the gospel).

Places most, if not all, the focus of the church is on the now, forgetting the eternal.

The Corrective — When you see someone in need, help ease the burdens of others. Justice is about making things right for people, destroying the oppressive structures that hold people in bondage. The opposite of justice is found in the Pharisees. Jesus tells the crowd, "They crush you with impossible religious demands and never lift a finger to help ease the burden" (Matthew 23:4).

James tells us "Suppose you see a brother or sister who needs food or clothing, and you say, "Well, good-bye and God bless you; stay warm and eat well"—but then you don't give that person any food or clothing. What good does that do? So you see, it isn't enough just to have faith. Faith that doesn't show itself by good deeds is no faith at all—it is dead and useless" (2:15-17).

The fullness and, dare we say, balance of love is most clearly witnessed when the three sides of love — grace, truth, and justice are present and fully functioning. The tension or polarities must be allowed to exist so that the fullness of love can be experienced and lived out in our personal and corporate lives as believers.

Another example of how our view of God impacts our theology is in knowing truth. Knowing truth has been the pursuit of great thinkers of every century. Exactly how we come to know this truth is another matter. The natural (modernistic/scientific/institutional) approach will argue that truth can be verified (which is true) and must be studied through scientific means — truth is an object to know, resulting in propositions and principles to be known, understood, and applied. What is then true is true for all, an absolute. Truth is then something that is studied and verified. An "it" or "object" that can be described, studied, and explained. It is hard to have a relationship with an "it" or an "object", but one can access the necessary principles from the study to apply to whatever situation that is deemed appropriate. Again, this field of endeavor is not wrong, but without the compliment of the polarity, it is incomplete.

On the other hand, the postmodern (relational/personal/dynamic) will argue that truth cannot be verified in a laboratory but must be experienced personally — truth is encountered. Again, this is true. What is true is then what is true for me, no absolutes (obviously an oxymoron — to argue there is no absolute truth is an absolute truth). On the one hand, the natural person takes truth and objectifies it. While the postmodern, on the other hand, will take truth and subjectify it with the inherent danger of subjectivism, which is the position that truth is nothing more than one's subjective response or action. Truth is then a subject to be encountered, to be known, and experienced. Both approaches are right and wrong at the same time. They need each other, just like the right and left brain need each other to function properly.

The Church has tried to understand the postmodern swing in our western culture. Some marvelous books have been written on the cultural shift (which continues to shift). It is rather ironic that so much would be written on something that is so hard to define and continuously changing. It still seems to these writers that attempts by the Church to understand postmodernity have been nothing more than stylistic reactions to a changing culture. As a result, we offer more relational settings (round tables and coffee — Starbucks of course), visual aids, movie clips, etc., to engage our MTV entrenched society. All of which have been good for the Church to employ in its attempts to reach our culture. However, if postmodernism is a reaction to modernity and the enlightenment, then our attempts to provide a more understandable and relevant Church service for the new generation of people is a noble but futile attempt.

We applaud the attempts the Church of the 21st Century has taken to be relevant. Trying to communicate the gospel in the language and style of the people is an important and necessary endeavor. That is, if such attempts are based in the relevance of language and style only. All too often what seems to happen is the church loses its spiritual identity as it blends far too much with the culture to the point that we are not only relevant in our language and style, but in morality as well. The late Henri Nouwen takes his ecclesiological boat and paddles upstream against the flow of current thought as he speaks prophetically and challenges the church of today. "I am deeply convinced that the Christian leader of the future is called to be completely irrelevant and to stand in this world with nothing to offer but his or her own vulnerable self. That is the way Jesus came to reveal God's love." (*In The Name of Jesus*, Crossroad, New York, 1997, p. 17).

The human heart is longing for something more than fabricated religion. God might be a God of order but He is not a God that is predictable. Lucy, in C. S. Lewis' classic, *The Lion, The Witch, and the Wardrobe*, asks Mr. Beaver if Aslan, the lion (figure of Christ) is safe. Mr. Beaver responds by saying that the great Aslan is not safe, but he is good. The human creation of a god is one in which he is predictable and controlled by righteous behavior that will guarantee blessing and a lifetime of security. And yet, the deeper longings of our postmodern generation seem to be expressing a desire for something more than what the Church so often provides. Thousands, if not millions, are looking for a God-encounter, a supernatural experience that would add life and even playful unpredictability (the delightful surprises of life that tend to be eliminated when we live lives of control and security) to a rather dull and predictable world, which can lead to a world that is rather hopeless, mundane, and without purpose.

Albert Camus (born in Algeria in 1913 and died in France in 1960) captured despair and hopelessness in his reworking of the classical myth by Homer called **"Sisyphus."** This is a story of Sisyphus who had died and gone to the nether world. He was sent back to earth. When recalled to the nether world he refused to return, for he so enjoyed the pleasures of earth. As punishment he was sentenced to push a large rock to the top of a hill. Whenever he would get to the top of the hill the rock would roll back down. He would trudge his way to the bottom of the hill and begin to the push the rock back up the hill. He was doomed to repeat this process endlessly. For all his efforts there was no permanent resolve. In the same vein, Camus correlates the workman of today who works every day at the same tasks, and his fate is no less absurd. Getting up at the same time everyday to deal with the same things every day only to go to bed at night and discover that the next day is the same as the last. Life seems like nothing more than constant maintenance; a chasing after something that will never be there. Our world is hungry and ripe for an encounter with the living God.

In simple language, unless we provide a place for people to encounter God, as we are encountering Him, then we have done nothing more than creative marketing that has forgotten to provide a quality product. The Church is then analogous to a family that provides a wonderful meal for their neighborhood. They invite everyone to come for dinner. As people walk in they smell the delightful aroma of a home cooked meal, enjoy the ambiance provided by the followers, the music and the warm greeting by the members of the family. The embrace is so loving and the feeling of belonging and acceptance is near perfect. The anticipation grows for the meal, light snacks are provided to help curb the appetite and build towards the main course. To the surprise of the guests no meal is served. Rather it is described in great detail with PowerPoint presentations and even a movie clip that enriches the picture of the meal for the hearers. The guests leave the house with a great idea of what the meal is but still find themselves hungry. Although the service and hospitality at the house were great, near perfect, it did not meet the great need of hunger within; and so, the guests go elsewhere in search of food to satisfy their hunger.

In our modern day churches we often have the relational dynamics down (the ambiance, mood altering worship, technology, relevant sermons, etc.,) but we forget to provide the actual meal — the stuff that actually makes us the Church — the atmosphere where a real life God-encounter can take place and people can feast on the Lord to satisfy the deeper spiritual hunger of their souls. People don't go to a sports bar to watch soap operas. Since we are the Church, maybe we should not hold back on what we do so that people will encounter God as He is. It's one thing for people to come to our churches and leave hungry because we do not provide a meal. It is entirely another for people to come to our churches and experience the meal and find themselves with a choice to eat or not. At least if they leave hungry, they do so because they chose to reject the Lord.

Enough of our soapbox; let us return to our delightful discussion of knowing truth. There is a sense where studying a geological formation or the potential of water on Mars is an objective endeavor. It is obviously an object that needs to be analyzed, understood, explained, and categorized. The scientific community and much of our analytical processes in various fields of research have yielded a great deal of knowledge that has helped us in this biosphere called earth. Utilizing the laboratory and objective research is not the issue, but the polarization of a methodology or a viewpoint is.

We tend to polarize ourselves on one side or the other. For example, the lens by which we view God and life affects us at every point, which often causes us to completely reject the opposing viewpoint. After all, we cannot see what the other viewpoint sees with the lens we are wearing. It is true that truth is a principle that can be known and an experience that must be encountered. Both are necessary. Truth will be true in every situation, but unless I experience it's reality, it won't be a truth for me.

With that said, let us process just how the polarization of our viewpoints, when it comes to God, can and does undermine the very fabric of our Christian faith and practice and is perhaps the resulting cause of why we are so impotent (overall) in our Western world to reach a world that is spiritually hungry but not so eager to check out our wonderful church services.

Every viewpoint, if polarized, limits itself in understanding the nature and essence of God. Liberal faith (Ethical Christianity), for example, emphasizes God the Father (the source) and focuses its energies on ethical and social matters, tending to be syncretistic in its theology and practice. Those who utilize this lens tend to view God and life in a more ethical and social context and see God as a principle that is demonstrated in service (the social gospel).

Salvation or Evangelical Christianity would center itself on the atoning and saving work of the cross through the resurrected Christ. The key component of this view is its emphasis on right doctrine. Truth, in this camp, has been regulated as a propositional reality (the bread and butter of "Fundamentalist" Christianity). The emphasis of such a faith is on a correct view of God (correct doctrine), the infallibility of the Bible (right belief will result in the Word of God speaking to you), right doctrinal belief will result in living right, and applying a proven church growth method will automatically result in church growth. Although Jesus is the center of this theological construct, and should be, the tendency is for truth to be reduced to principle rather than housed and made real in the person of Christ. The Word of God becomes the rulebook that judges every action (again a correct under-standing but without a concept of the relational reality of God, this belief turns the life-giving Scripture into a wooden book of rules and truth propositions that provides a judicial sense of those who are in — living right — and those who are out — living wrong). Truth is both propositional and housed in a person (Christ), making it personal. God, as person, existed prior to creation and therefore for us to know truth propositions, we must first know the Person from which all truth propositions flow. To begin with, the truth as a statement or proposition misses the reality of the incarnation, the "Immanuel" in Christ.

To know the Way, one must come to know the Person of Jesus, since Jesus, the Person, is the Way.

Spiritual or Experiential Christianity (the relational view) would argue for experience, emphasizing the person and work of the Holy Spirit over propositional truth, spirituality over right doctrine, and spontaneity over structure. The lens by which this position views God and life is experiential. Truth is an experiential reality that cannot be confined to a laboratory or defined adequately. At best, it can be described much like the function of a narrative (like Luke wrote in the Book of Acts regarding the day of Pentecost). Narratives are meant to be experienced; a story told that communicates the experience of a person or a group. The danger here is that experience becomes the almighty criterion, which if left to itself opens up a Pandora's box of theological mayhem that leaves personal experience as the ultimate guide to truth (solipsism).

It is apparent that the polarities must be synthesized and when we do, we come to see the fullness of God. Truth is then an object that can be studied and even verified, a subject that is known as one would know another person, and an experience that must be encountered for it to be true for me. It is not one aspect but involves the whole. Hence, we come to know the truth as a person first (Christ, the Immanuel, incarnate in our midst), which is verified and/or illuminated through the written word of God by the Holy Spirit, and made real as we experience the person of Jesus through the Holy Spirit.

When it comes to God it is important that we not reduce Him to some "cosmic force," "principle" (to live by), or "power." Evangelical Christianity would cringe at such a thought, and yet so much of what we seem to practice as Christianity centers around right principles for living that reduces God to a "principle" or "power." The Bible makes it quite clear that God is a person. If God were nothing more than a philosophical category, like so many make Him out to be, then the most suitable way to know Him would be through intellectual reflection. If God is nothing more than a "cosmic principle" then all one needs is a right understanding of what the principle is and how to live according to it. If God were some cosmic power source that can be tapped, then the mode by which we access God (the activation code) becomes a necessary aspect to our spirituality and prayer finds itself reduced to incantations that look and sound a lot like magic. Underlying each category is the irony of the self that seeks to serve something greater than itself and while so doing ends up creating a god in its own image. Control, security, and self-idolization are the fundamental realities of our human existence and polarized views of God allow us to have some sense (although not real) of control, security, and self-idolization.

God is a person, and if this is the case, then all of our attempts to systematize and study Him will not necessarily yield the fruit of intimate knowledge that only comes from knowing the person. Facts about a person are not the same as knowing the person. Simply, you discover Truth when you discover the Person. We are not arguing against a systematic representation of God such as systematic theology, but simply clarifying that knowing facts about a person and knowing the person are not necessarily the same thing. Reflection upon our experience, seeking to understand our relationship more so that we might glorify God more in our lives and our churches, is the purpose behind any theological enterprise.

To the Jews who had believed him, Jesus said, "If you hold to my teaching, you are really my disciples. Then you will know the truth, and the truth will set you free." (John 8:31-32)

How You Come to Know the Life: In Community

You *discover* Life when you discover the Person.

"The thief comes only to steal and kill and destroy; I have come that they may have life, and have it to the full." (John 10:10)

One of the more discouraging realities in our church world today is that so many seem to live far less than the abundant life that is boldly promised by Jesus. He has come to not only give life but lavish us with it; and yet so many seem to live far below the promise. We are not arguing for the "higher life" here or perfectionism, but simply making an observation about the status of so many Christian lives. Maybe one of the causes of our lackluster faith is that we do not know how to exist in community. Receiving salvation is only half of the reality of the redeemed life. Martin Luther, the great reformer, described his process as leaving the world to find God only to find that gracious God he longed to find would not allow him to hide in isolation but sent him back to the world. If we are going to live the life of Jesus then we must find it in the Person of Christ and the persons that make up the body of Christ.

Life is nothing more than relationship. First, there is relationship with God. We come to know ourselves only as we come to know God. We are not the "I Am" as noted earlier. We are dependent beings (the penultimate) and must have a power source to operate. God is that power source and we can only survive fully when we are plugged in (Acts 17:28) and that plug in is the Cross and Person of Jesus.

The second is then relationship with the self. That's right, not with others, but with the self. As we discover who God is we discover who we are. As John Calvin so wonderfully stated "It is certain that man never achieves a clear knowledge of himself unless he has first looked upon God's face, and then descends from contemplating him to scrutinize himself. For we always seem to ourselves righteous and upright and wise and holy — this pride is innate in all of us — unless by clear proofs we stand convinced of our own unrighteousness, foulness, folly, and impurity. Moreover, we are not thus convinced if we look merely to ourselves and not also to the Lord, who is the sole standard by which this judgment must be measured." (*Institutes of the Christian Religion*, Bk. 1, chap. 1.2, p. 37). After all, we are called to love others as we love ourselves. Salvation in that sense not only causes new life ("born again"), but brings a sense of harmony to our broken world of emotional torment (struggle with personal identity), restoring the Imago Dei. We can only love others after we have experienced love (I John 4:19).

The third relational category is then relationship with others. This is where our discussion will focus as it pertains to Jesus as the Life. We come to know life best in community, in relationship with others. Dietrich Bonhoeffer goes so far as to say: "The Church is the Church only when it exists for others. . . The Church must share in the secular problems of ordinary human life, not dominating, but helping and serving. It must tell men of every calling what it means to live in Christ, to exist for others." (*Letters and Papers from Prison*, p. 211) We find life more alive and dynamic when we are in relationship with others, incarnating the gospel, pitching our tent and living amongst others.

There is a sense where personal identity is discovered in relationship first with God and then with others (I-Thou). After all, you can't know if you are dark, tall, handsome, etc., unless there is another. In that way, the "I" is developed in relationship with others, the "thou." Living in community is then an excellent way for us to discover our imperfections. It reveals our weaknesses, helping us to deepen our humility, which is fundamental to life in Christ. Hidden faults are more easily observed by others than by ourselves.

Living life with others is no easy task as is evidenced by the constant relational struggle that exists. The truth is that when two objects become close friction will take place. The wise sage of Proverbs states it this way, "As iron sharpens iron, a friend sharpens a friend." (27:17). Friction is a natural result of closeness, which translated into relational vernacular means conflict is inevitable. The issue is not that conflict takes place but how we handle conflict. If you are having conflict in your church, staff, relationships, etc., be encouraged. It means that the avenue of closeness is upon you. The art of navigating through such becomes the key to deepening our lives in Christ and with others as we learn to live this life together.

A wise hermit said: "Whoever lives with brothers should not be as the sharp stone with jagged edges, but rather as the round and smooth one, in order to remain similar to the others. I am here in the desert, not because I have many virtues, but due to my spiritual infirmity and weakness. Those who are strong live in the midst of others." May we all find the strength to live together as Christ so desired and modeled with His community of disciples so that the world will see a visible representation of Christ in His Church.

But *the knowledge of* the Way, the Truth and the Life is not enough. The goal is to have the wisdom of the Way, the wisdom embodied in the Person who is the Truth, so that we might apprehend and appropriate for ourselves the abundance of Him. To do that one must *encounter* the Person. Not just once, but in a continuing epic saga, a life-long journey of relationship and discovery of this one Person.

Jews demand miraculous signs and Greeks look for wisdom, but we preach Christ crucified: a stumbling block to Jews and foolishness to Gentiles, but to those whom God has called, both Jews and Greeks, Christ the power of God and the wisdom of God (1 Corinthians 1:22-25).

We will now expand on this idea of community in Part III.

PART 3

Our Community

☦

CHAPTER SEVEN

"THE REIGN OF GOD — HIS KINGDOM AND COMMUNITY"

Building on our understanding of **Our God** and **Ourselves**, what then, is the Church? Our journey of rediscovery brings us to the place that we must review our ecclesiology. Indeed, so far in this journey we have touched often upon the issue of "Church." Understanding the Church as community is essential to seeing how we reflect the nature of God. In His tri-unity He is Himself community. In the Trinity there is an economy of relationships. How then does that become expressed in the church?

"What life have you if you have not life together?

There is no life that is not in community,

And no community not lived in praise of God."

(T. S. Eliot, "Choruses from 'The Rock,'" in the *Complete Poems and Plays* 1909-1950)

What this simply tells us is that we receive life, we foster life, and we pass life on in the context of human relationships. Paul D. Hanson makes the bold statement that "Jesus did not organize an institution. Rather, He conformed His life completely to His vision of the order that He believed alone could create true community among humans and true harmony throughout creation." (*The People Called*, p. 428) The order Jesus is referring to is the "Kingdom of God." This order is made up of those who have submitted to His reign as the central reality of their lives.

One cannot talk about the Church or community without a discussion about the Kingdom of God. That is, God's reign, sovereignty, and dominion. Before we go on, it would be helpful if we took a moment to define what we mean by the Kingdom of God. We are greatly indebted to George Eldon Ladd and his work on the Kingdom of God. First, it is important to note that the Kingdom of God is not primarily concerned about *individual salvation*, but *the corporate mission* of the Church to see God's Kingdom established on earth. It's about God's rule. The Kingdom of God is then a realm people can enter "now" and a realm that is "not yet" fully realized, but will come in full glory and power. One enters the Kingdom of God in the "now" not through right-eous deeds, but by humbly receiving God's rule as one submits the self in absolute trust to God's rulership. Jesus teaches that:

He will give you all you need from day to day if you live for him and make the Kingdom of God your primary concern. (Matthew 6:33, NLT)

If one is living for the Kingdom of God then the rule of God is evident in the life of the loyal servant who seeks God's righteousness (His rule and reign in our lives).

The basic meaning of the Hebrew word *malkuth* in the Old Testament and the Greek word *basileia* in the New Testament involves the rank, authority, and sovereignty exercised by a king. The essential meaning when dealing with the Kingdom of God is then His reign, His universal rule. When we speak of the Kingdom of God we are talking about three things: God's reign (His right to rule) — His sovereign dominion over all that is, the realm of His Kingdom, and the "already and not yet" aspect of God's Kingdom (there is a Kingdom now, but one that is yet to come). When Jesus began to preach, this was the message He brought forth — a declaration of God's right to rule on Earth. The Rebellion was coming to an end, and the beginning of God's Kingdom had "come near" (Mark 1:14-15). This is the core of the Gospel message, with salvation for humankind an element and benefit of that rule.

The significance of the Kingdom of God for our discussion is its demand upon the life of the believing saint. Jesus radically altered the lives of His disciples from the very beginning by asking them to leave all they had and follow Him. His call today is no less demanding and radical. God does not ask us to find our righteousness on our own, He promises to give it to us. God's Kingdom does not ask us to create life or even to achieve a standard before we can receive it. Rather, God simply asks us to receive (respond) His gracious provision by submitting to His rule and reign. It is then that all will be added. Jesus declared early in His ministry that the way one receives the Kingdom is by repentance:

Turn from your sins and turn to God, because the Kingdom of Heaven is near. (Matthew 4:17)

Simply, one must repent, turn, and then decide to allow God's reign in their heart. As they receive it they receive the life it brings, the blessings it provides, and the wonderful destiny that awaits those who embrace it. We must all face the question:

"Jesus Christ is Lord. Now what are you going to do about it?"

The problem that many have within the realm of today's Christian society is that we have not allowed ourselves to be crucified with Christ. We often choose self-advancement over the Kingdom of God. When such takes place in the life of a believer, love for the things of God begins to die. This is all too evident as pastors and leaders carry on their ministries as if the ministries actually belong to them. The Bible seems to argue rather clearly that we are "stewards" (I Corinthians 4:1-2) or "managers" of our Master's affairs. No matter how great or awesome one's church or ministry might be, we are all just "servants" of the One who brings us life.

The nominal state of so many believers, including pastors and leaders, is alarming and even discouraging. Embracing God's rule in our lives, becoming radical and real followers of Christ, involves taking up one's cross. Jesus said,

If any of you wants to be my follower, you must put aside your selfish ambition, shoulder your cross daily, and follow me. (Luke 9:23)

Exactly what does it mean to "take up one's cross?" So much of what we call crosses in our Christian vernacular have nothing to do with the Cross that Jesus referred to. For example, our problems with people, trials, sicknesses, etc., might be difficult matters for us in life, but have very little to do with taking up your cross. The Cross is not a burden. Rather, it is a place of death. When one is willing to take up the Cross, they are ready to die. We are not talking about denying oneself of various things (as good as this is for practicing spiritual discipline), but to deny oneself — to give up rulership of your life and submit to the one who is King. Self-denial is centered upon the self; to deny the self is centered upon Christ. It is the language of personal death to one's dreams, ambitions, and desires. Cross-bearing deals with the question of lordship, rulership, and kingship. Christ cannot rule in my life until I count myself dead, crucified with Him. As Paul boldly asserts,

I myself no longer live, but Christ lives in me. So I live my life in this earthly body by trusting in the Son of God, who loved me and gave himself for me. (Galatians 2:20)

Practically, this means that we do not dictate to God the terms of our life, ministry or our involvement. The "I don't do windows" mentality that is so often found in the household of the faith. It's almost as if our gift assessments and personal mission statements have allowed us to skirt the issue of being servants. "I am a servant, but I just don't do windows. I can serve in the following ways based upon my gifts and personal mission statement." Now before you decide to blow a fuse, we are all for gift assessments and discovering your personal mission statement. Just take a moment to reflect on how such practices, without serious cross-bearing will lead to a language of biblical faith without the love and humility of biblical faith. When such transpires, we have those who serve only when it is within their comfort or best interest. After all, if it doesn't fit my personal mission statement or gifts, then I simply do not have to do it.

The Church of today has all the right pieces: the word of God, people, structure, prayer, motivation, money, and facilities. But are we putting them together correctly? It would be like having an incorrect original that one makes photocopies from — every copy would contain the error. We sometimes wonder if our church system is like photocopying — we simply make copies of what we think works without seeking God for what He might want to do in us and through us. Through us — doing "church" without Kingdom rule or cross-bearing.

Church is too much like watching the physical fitness programs of Tae Bo or Denise Austin on your television set. You never get in shape by simply watching them. You may learn all the moves, have understanding about physical fitness, and even have strong convictions about why people should do your type of training. But no matter how much you share your knowledge, the truth of your fitness still remains the same — you are not in shape. The Church of today "takes the redeemed sinners and forms them into a harmless species of polite churchgoers and program participants" (Wolfgang Simson, *Houses That Change The World*, p. 28)

Robert Banks helps us here by stating: "If only Christians were willing to be more with each other and corporately with God, they would find that although they do less, they actually achieve more." The key then is helping people learn **to be more** and not simply **to do more**. The question of the hour is how do we achieve this? Three things are essential to the life of those called into the kingdom community:

Be in relationship with God — Spiritual Vitality/Being With God (Mark 12:30-31);

Be in relationship with each other — Relational Priority/Being With Others (I Peter 1:22; I Corinthians 12:25; Galatians 6:2) and;

As you live your life, make disciples — Social Ministry/Being For Others (Matthew 28:19-20).

"The Church is the Church only when it exists for others. To make a start, it should give away all its property to those in need. The clergy must live solely on the free-will offerings of their congregations, or possibly engage in some secular calling. The Church must share in the secular problems of ordinary human life, not dominating, but helping and serving. It must tell men of every calling what it means to live in Christ, to exist for others." (Dietrich Bonhoeffer, *Letters and Papers from Prison*, p. 211) This is a radical statement from a radical man who believed that when "Christ calls a man, He bids him come and die." (*The Cost of Discipleship*, p. 7) We are not asking you to agree with the totality of Bonhoeffer's statement, but to wrestle with the relational paradigm he set forth and that we have been contending for in this book.

The response of any faithful disciple is not a proper confession of faith (as right as this is), but an act of obedience. Like the first disciples, Jesus called them and they responded by following Him. True discipleship begins with the living Christ as we follow His kingly rule and base our lives upon it. Christianity without discipleship is Christianity without Christ.

Obedience based on our confession of faith takes us beyond simple belief into a spiritually-empowered missional reality. The obedient disciple shares the *words of Jesus (go and tell)* and also does the *works of Jesus (go and do)*. John Wimber explained that the *words* of Jesus (the Gospel) *illustrate* the truth of the Kingdom rule of God, while the *works* of Jesus *demonstrate* the truth and reality of God's authority and dominion. For example, through the parables of the Kingdom in Matthew 13 Jesus explained to us what the kingdom of God is like. To mankind, caught within the fallen spiritual blindness of our world, He uses these wonderful word-pictures to illustrate the Kingdom reality to us. We cannot see it without spiritual re-birth, so He describes it to us. His powerful works then demonstrate for us the reality of the resurgence of God's Kingdom rule on earth through Christ, as He destroys the Devil's work in the lives of men and women (1 John 3:8b). Such mission — in both words and works — is integral to the life of the Kingdom community known as the Church. Indeed, it is to be the everyday reality of our lives, and comes as the result of lives submitted to His kingdom rule.

Elements of the Kingdom Community

What then, are the hallmarks of this Kingdom Community? When I see it, how will I know it? What are the essential elements that comprise it? Three things stand out: *incarnation*, *proclamation* and *demonstration*.

Incarnation: Living the Truth (The Gift of Presence)

Jesus became flesh (John 1:14) and "pitched his tent" among us. Jesus is the living Word that is the gift from God the Father — the gift of presence. "But now in these final days, he has spoken to us through his Son. God promised everything to the Son as an inheritance, and through the Son He made the universe and everything in it. The Son reflects God's own glory, and everything about Him represents God exactly (Hebrews 1:2-3).

Life is incarnational and about impartation. Like God with Adam, we are to impart life to others. Obviously, we are not speaking of doing so in like fashion, but metaphorically. And so, to "pitch one's tent" is to live with and among others so that they might experience and encounter the reality of God in the totality of our lives.

Our age is essentially a dialogue of the deaf. The best way to speak to deaf hearts is by incarnating the gospel or giving the gift of presence. The gift of presence is often best served by listening. A key for community development is to cultivate the art of listening to what a person's heart is saying - not just their words.

For leadership to be life-giving and long-lasting, it must be incarnational in nature. An old adage typifies this point: "Every man has three names; one his father and mother give him; one others call him; and one he acquires himself." Incarnational leadership means one must lead primarily out of who one is and not simply what one knows, who one knows, what one can do, or how one can do it. Henri Nouwen says it well: "Christian leadership is not a leadership of power and control, but a leadership of powerlessness and humility in which the suffering servant of God, Jesus Christ, is made manifest. We, obviously, are not speaking about a psychologically weak leadership in which the Christian leader is simply the passive victim of the manipulations of his milieu. No, I am speaking of a leadership in which power is constantly abandoned in favor of love." (*In The Name of Jesus*, p. 63) We are then to be just like Jesus who became a man, humbling Himself and being of no reputation, and being obedient to the point of death. Unless we allow the power of God to impact us, the reality of His presence will be circumvented. Jesus must be in us in order for Him to be given away.

It is precisely the lack of humility before God that is the root cause of nearly all leadership problems. For example, if the power resources transcend the character strength of the individual, collapse or a moral lapse is inevitable. Simply, God does not work through us greatly until we recognize our impotence. The lyrics of an old song reinforce this point, "If you want to be great in God's Kingdom learn to be the servant of all."

Proclamation: Speaking the Truth with Others

Nicolaus Copernicus (1473-1543) changed the way we view our universe and our planet. Up until that time the Ptolemaic view was the standard view of the day, including philosophers and mainline science. This view held that the Earth was the center of the universe, meaning the Sun and the planets orbited around the Earth. Copernicus came along and reversed this by postulating that the sun was the center of our universe (the principle of heliocentric planetary motion). All of this to say, we are not the center of the universe nor am "I" the center of the universe. In simple language, this universe or world is not about me. This is a critical concept to grasp if we are going to understand what it means to live in the Image of God. Like the moon, we are lesser orbs, orbiting around the sun, revealing its brilliant light. The light we have is not our own (we are dependent beings), but the light of the sun. And in the same way, we are reflecting the light of our Lord, the Son, who is at the center of life's universe (cf. Ephesians 1:20-22). We are mirrors reflecting the brilliance of our God.

But whenever anyone turns to the Lord, then the veil is taken away. Now, the Lord is the Spirit, and wherever the Spirit of the Lord is, he gives freedom. And all of us have had that veil removed so that we can be mirrors that brightly reflect (or so that we can see in a mirror) the glory of the Lord. And as the Spirit of the Lord works within us, we become more and more like him and reflect his glory even more. (I Corinthians 3:16-18)

The key to reflection is found in one word, *behold*. The mirror can only reflect that which it beholds. Our lives reflect what we behold. If our lives are reflecting Christ, then something of "love, joy, peace, etc. (Galatians 5:22-23) should be evident in our lives.

Not only are we to live the Gospel in front of others, but we are also to tell them about the grace and wonder of Jesus (Romans 10:14-15; I Peter 3:15). It is true that the Church is called to proclaim the gospel with more than just words. Our very lives are to be a proclamation. Proclamation is something we do from the substance of our lives, e.g., lights give off light and so we should give off Jesus.

Demonstration: Living/Giving the Truth for Others — A Life That Reveals Christ

The focus here is on works and active demonstration, the social gospel and the Gospel demonstrated in works of power. James makes it clear that faith without demonstration is a dead faith.

Dear brothers and sisters, what's the use of saying you have faith if you don't prove it by your actions? That kind of faith can't save anyone. Suppose you see a brother or sister who needs food or clothing, and you say, 'Well, good-bye and God bless you; stay warm and eat well'–but then you don't give that person any food or clothing. What good does that do? So you see, it isn't enough just to have faith. Faith that doesn't show itself by good deeds is no faith at all–it is dead and useless. (James 2:14-17)

In summary, the Gospel is incarnational. It must take on human form. In this sense the Gospel is private and must personally impact us so that it is in us. As we have said before, "what we are when we are alone with God is really what makes up the substance of our faith." The aspect of proclamation must be part and parcel of our Christianity, for we are not to hide what we have. Jesus tells us that we

are the light of the world. A city built on a hill cannot be hid. No one after hiding a lamp puts it under a bushel basket, but on the lampstand, and it gives light to all in the house. In the same way, let your light shine before others, so that they may see your good works and give glory to your Father in heaven. (Matthew 5:14-16)

The teaching of Jesus also captures the essence of demonstration. We are to be visible with our faith and do things that demonstrate the reign of God in our lives by actions that will cause people to give praise to God

(Matthew 5:16; 25:31-46; Galatians 6:2; James 2:14-26; I Peter 2:12, 15). Faith may be an invisible matter, but its expression is definitely visible. We can go so far as to say, "if we can't see your faith, then you don't have any faith." This can also be said of love.

From here, we will look at the nature of this Kingdom community and how it affects the practice of our life and faith.

CHAPTER EIGHT

"THE CHURCH AS A FAMILY"

Thinking about being part of the universal Kingdom community can be overwhelming and even feel a bit impersonal. (All this theology can tend to leave one a bit cold!) The self does not lose significance in the scope of the whole. Indeed, it gains transcendence through it. Yet, understanding that the Kingdom community is also a *family with a mission* is essential in maintaining proper perspective. The essential elements of the mission (*incarnation, proclamation and demonstration*) can only truly occur in a relational context.

Church *Imago Dei*

The Church — this Kingdom community made in His image as individuals and as a whole — is far more than just an organization. It is a living organism. It cannot be a machine or structure or institution any more than its Creator can be such things. It is something more than just an empty form — it is something which is alive. Yet most people today have a variety of definitions of what "church" is. Some think of a white building with a steeple on top, others may think of it as an institution, an organization with its committees, programs, and budgets.

Most think of a church as being a place, the "house of God," in which Christians gather for religious activities. Indeed, this is what the English word "church" means — "the Lord's house." It comes from the Middle English word *chirche*, from Old English *cirice*, ultimately from Medieval Greek *kurikon*, from Late Greek *kuriakon (doma)*, the Lord's (house). Even here the connotation is people who belong to the Lord, and yet over the centuries it has been transformed to mean a place or building.

We have spoken before of the Greek word for "church" that Jesus uses in Matthew 16:18, "ekklesia," which means *"a called-out assembly, a congregation set apart."* From this we can see the perspective of what Jesus meant when He said that He would build His Church. The church that Jesus was speaking of was His people, described as "the Church which is His Body"

(Ephesians 1:23). Therefore, the Church in all of its diverse and many expressions is called to be one people of God, not a place or building.

In the Gospels Jesus goes beyond the broader concept of the Church as God's representative people (which implies a task orientation) into a deeper and richer, more relational context — the Church as the family of Father God.

What defines this family? The word "family" has various meanings to people, dependant upon culture and personal experience. Some have a well-defined view of what family is; to others family is a very loosely-framed idea. We gain insight into Jesus' viewpoint on this issue from Matthew 12:46-50:

But he replied to the man who told him, "Who is my mother, and who are my brothers?" And stretching out his hand toward his disciples, he said, "Here are my mother and my brothers! For whoever does the will of my Father in heaven is my brother, and sister, and mother.

Clearly, Jesus was saying that His true kindred were composed of those individuals who had in common God as their Father. It is common parentage which defines the Church as a family, a common Imago Dei. It is not doctrine or tradition or sacramental practices — it is the one primary Parent that we have in common. All who are born anew from above by His Holy Spirit are part of this family (John 3:3-8) and share in the image and nature of the Father.

Even more — we are not just individual children, but an interconnected and interdependent family:

So then you are no longer strangers and sojourners, but you are fellow citizens with the saints and members of the household of God, built upon the foundation of the apostles and prophets, Christ Jesus himself being the cornerstone, in whom the whole structure is joined together and grows into a holy temple in the Lord; in whom you also are built into it for a dwelling place of God in the Spirit. (Ephesians 2:19-22 RSV)

This one family, indwelt by the Holy Spirit becomes the New Temple, the place in which God's glory dwells. Paul tells us that this family is named by Him (Ephesians 3:14-15). In other words, it gains its identity (both the corporate whole and the individuals who comprise it) from He who is the Father. Paul continues to indicate that we must continue in unity as there is but one Church family, as there is only one Father:

Make every effort to keep the unity of the Spirit in the bond of peace. There is one Body and one Spirit — just as you were called to one hope when you were called — one Lord, one faith, one baptism; one God and Father of us all, who is over all and through all and in all. (Ephesians 4:3-6)

The passage from Ephesians 2 quoted above, along with 1 Peter 2:2-10 points out the fact that we are being fit together upon the foundation of Christ to become one whole. In Christ the diversity of many individuals is formed into but one totality.

Like newborn babes, long for the pure spiritual milk, that by it you may grow up to salvation; for you have tasted the kindness of the Lord. Come to him, to that living stone, rejected by men but in God's sight chosen and precious; and like living stones be yourselves built into a spiritual house, to be a holy priesthood, to offer spiritual sacrifices acceptable to God through Jesus Christ. For it stands in scripture: "Behold, I am laying in Zion a stone, a cornerstone chosen and precious, and he who believes in him will not be put to shame." To you therefore who believe, he is precious, but for those who do not believe, "The very stone which the builders rejected has become the head of the corner," and "A stone that will make men stumble, a rock that will make them fall"; for they stumble because they disobey the word, as they were destined to do. But you are a chosen race, a royal priesthood, a holy nation, God's own people, that you may declare the wonderful deeds of him who called you out of darkness into his marvelous light. Once you were no people but now you are God's people; once you had not received mercy but now you have received mercy. (1 Peter 2:2-10 NIV)

A Family Called to Oneness in Him

What is the foundation on which the Church is built? The passages which we just read show us that in the person of Jesus Christ, the Son of the Father, we are formed and knit together by the one Holy Spirit — the Triune God at work in His family. All who take part in the New Covenant are joined together with each other through the body and blood of Jesus (John 6:53-66). The greatest desire that the Father has for His family is that through Jesus we might be unified perfectly. This was His prayer for us in John 17:

My prayer is not for them alone. I pray also for those who will believe in me through their message, that all of them may be one, Father, just as you are in me and I am in you. May they also be in us so that the world may believe that you have sent me. I have given them the glory that you gave me, that they may be one as we are one: I in them and you in me. May they be brought to complete unity to let the world know that you sent me and have loved them even as you have loved me.

The unity and oneness which God desires for His family is of no less degree than the unity and oneness found within the Trinity. The accord which is in God Himself is the accord which He longs for in His people. Again, Imago Dei — His image in us. His diversity expressed, bounded by His love. This unity to which we are called can only occur when we have completely committed to Christ and to His people. We must allow koininia to be the organizing principle of our life. As we are members of His family we cannot separate our commitment to Him and our commitment to each other, as it is part of our commitment to Him that we are called to love, care for, and uphold one another. His command to love one another leaves us no choice but to do so, as to be His disciples we are enjoined to keep His commandments.

Family Called to Commitment

As the Church is the Lord's family it is totally unique, different from any other group of people on the face of the earth. Unlike other human organizations, groups, clubs, or societies the Church is not based solely on a common purpose (although we do have a common purpose), but rather on a *common relationship with Jesus*. We share in a common family heritage: we are children of the Most High. Consequently, as our relationship with each other is founded on Jesus, as children of one Father, we have a deeper responsibility to the local church and to each other than those in human organizations. *This might best be described as Contribution vs. Commitment.*

A "contribution" can be either large or small, can happen on an occasional basis, and is something that one can leave behind. People contribute time, money, or personal effort on an "at will" basis to secular groups, and then can decide when they are done to freely walk away. A "commitment" goes beyond making occasional contributions, but is rather a regular and consistent effort to see something through to its completion.

To illustrate the difference between contribution and commitment, Tom loves to tell the "Chicken and Pig" story to his new member classes at his church. (He couldn't resist including it here.)

A chicken and a pig are walking down the street and see a sign in a diner window: "Bacon and Eggs — $1.99." The owner sees them and says, "Hey, I'm running low on supplies. How about some help?" The Chicken says, "Sure, I'll make a contribution" and proceeds to lay an egg for the man and walks away. The pig said "No way! For me to help you, I'd have to put my fat in the fire!" The pig got out of there as fast as he could. Helping the owner of the diner was easy for the chicken — all he had to do was make a contribution.

For the pig, it required a commitment.

Commitments cannot be just walked away from–you have to be willing to put your fat in the fire. Being part of the family of God, which is His Church, requires that people do more than just make a contribution, but rather that they be committed to the Lord, His family, and the work of the local church. As part of a local expression of the Church we are called to be committed to the individuals and families which comprise the larger family of that Church. We are called to interact with, love, encourage, support, and help provide for the needs of every person within the community of our local church, not on an occasional basis, but regularly and continually.

Here's a true story — no farm animals involved. Several brothers from a prominent family in a town decided that their town needed a new playground for the area children. Approaching the town fathers, they were told there was no budget for such a project. In response, they offered to raise both the funding and the labor to undertake the project if the town would provide the property. The town leaders agreed and a top-flight playground architect was engaged, and the playground project was underway. Financial contributions, both large and small, were gathered over time and the playground was funded. Then the work began. Much to the dismay of the brothers organizing the project, money was easier to find than helpers. They found themselves putting in hours of labor on the playground while others showed up randomly or not at all, and when they did come to work on the playground they would stay for an hour or two at most. Very often, after their short stint on the job, they would not even put away the tools they were using. Needless to say, the playground project did get completed — and it's a beauty, but it was completed by the commitment of the brothers and a few others like them, and not by the casual, random contributions of the townspeople.

The One Lord has one Church which is His one family, a family called to both unity and commitment. Again, this is reflective of His own oneness found within Himself.

The Church as Family and Individual Identity

Such a view of our relationship with God, e.g. the Church as a family, goes against the grain of many in the West. Our strong individualistic world view comes into conflict with such relational realities as "family," "unity," "inter-dependence" and being a *people* of God as opposed to being a *person* who belongs to God. In the Western paradigm, identity is drawn primarily from one's characteristics and abilities. The biblical view is that identity is drawn as part of a larger whole — a family, and more specifically, from our Father. Perhaps this is why so many Christians in our culture don't know their identity in Christ — they are not looking to their Father for identity, they are looking at themselves, and the self being inherently flawed leaves them with a flawed identity. Since the relational context of family is designed to be a formative tool for identity, our individualized quest for identity resists exterior definition of the self and we lose the benefit of Christ's formative work in our life through the Church community. This is truly a stronghold in our thinking (2 Corinthians 10:3-5) that resists the knowledge of Christ coming into us, specifically in the aspect of our identity as a child of the Father.

A Family with a Mission

Jesus gave His family a mission upon His ascent into heaven. Two passages, one from the Gospel of Matthew and another from the Book of the Acts of the Apostles shows us His expectation for us, a missional body.

Then Jesus came to them and said, 'All authority in heaven and on earth has been given to me. Therefore go and make disciples of all nations, baptizing them in the name of the Father and of the Son and of the Holy Spirit, and teaching them to obey everything I have commanded you. And surely I am with you always, to the very end of the age.' (Matthew 28:18-20)

This missional "Great Commission" has driven the extension efforts of the Church for 2,000 years. Sharing the words of Jesus and doing His works comprise the incarnational, global mandate of the Church. This mandate is to teach them what is commanded and how to live it — not just information, but modeling transformed lives, making disciples by teaching and demonstrating.

But you will receive power when the Holy Spirit comes on you; and you will be my witnesses in Jerusalem, and in all Judea and Samaria, and to the ends of the earth. Acts 1:8

Basically Jesus was telling His disciples *"You will reflect Me to the entire world through the grace empowerment of the Spirit."* Part of the Spirit's work would be to "manifest" (Gk. phanerosis — *show through*) Jesus to people through the indwelt Church. The Church would speak the words of Jesus by the Spirit and do the works of Jesus by the same Spirit. As discussed earlier, the two cannot be separated in the ministry of the Gospel of the Kingdom.

The Church within our culture has misunderstood the nature of this missional call, as if it is *something we do*. Rather the mission of the church is fulfilled as the Church lives as the Church. The mission proceeds from our *being together in Christ*, not our doing together. The *doing in Christ* is the outcome of the *being in Christ*. The focus is on being, as what you do in (for/through) Christ proceeds from your being in Him. Again, the issue is incarnation and submission to His Kingdom rule. Mission flows from these two things. That is koinonia, and that is the Fellowship of the Cross.

To describe the missional aspect of Christ reaching out to the world in reconciliation, Paul utilizes the concept of the Body of Christ. However, right now we need to say that this is more than an abstract concept, but a spiritual reality. From an incarnational viewpoint, Jesus lives in His Church today and ministers to the world through it. This Body is alive, indwelt and empowered by the Spirit of Christ. It is organic, always changing, always growing in some fashion.

Here is one major area the New Testament organic Church, His Body, His family, the kingdom community comes into conflict with the current Church reality in our culture. What we have today is more akin to a business or a machine as opposed to a living thing. Its produce is often inorganic and dead. Activity is portrayed as life. *A rose by any other name .... could be plastic!* Silk flowers are pretty and last a long time but they aren't real flowers, rather they are a substitute for the sake of convenience and economy. In the church in our culture today our fruit is often fake and our churches are simply like Styrofoam cups, a utilitarian tool meant to be discarded once it is used once.

In contrast, this missional aspect of the Church and indeed the Church itself is a living thing, Christ reaching out through us, with a genetic code that gives it a pattern for thriving health and unlimited growth. It is both sustainable in our day, and in its core design, is built to last the ages.

CHAPTER NINE

"THE CHURCH AS COMMUNITY"

Looking at the genetic code of the church in the New Testament

How, then, does this living, organic thing called the Church, this body with its many parts, this family with its relational fabric and nature; how does it also engage in the task-oriented aspect of mission? How does the incarnation, proclamation and demonstration spoken of earlier come together? A snapshot of the early church gives us some clues into how the living Church undertakes the activity of mission:

They devoted themselves to the apostles' teaching and to the fellowship, to the breaking of bread and to prayer. Everyone was filled with awe, and many wonders and miraculous signs were done by the apostles. All the believers were together and had everything in common. Selling their possessions and goods, they gave to anyone as he had need. Every day they continued to meet together in the temple courts. They broke bread in their homes and ate together with glad and sincere hearts, praising God and enjoying the favor of all the people. And the Lord added to their number daily those who were being saved. (Acts 2:42-47 NIV)

The young Church (which, in our view, was neither the "primitive church" nor the idyllic high watermark of the ages) lived life together, and the outflow of that shared life was the ministry of the Gospel. They lived, and ministry flowed from their life together. They were a *community*.

As shared earlier, one definition of community might be *"a shared life together."* Adding a common faith component, the definition of the Church as community could be *"a shared life together in Christ."* It is both natural and has purpose. It is how the fullness of organic life and task comes together. Community *combines* family and mission making the ministry of the Gospel "the family business," with each member of the community having a specific and significant role in the endeavor. Community is the highest and finest expression of koinonia in the Kingdom "now."

Community, this shared life together in Christ, becomes the backdrop of our existence — it informs everything. The relationship amongst the saints is the very fabric of life, and the outreach to those still outside the Kingdom community becomes a main organizing principle of that life. The community of the redeemed becomes that reflector of His glory — that incarnated light. It is the "City on a Hill" (Matthew 5), the loving arms and the healing hands of Jesus. It is through this community, sharing life in Him, that the world sees Jesus. Not through one but through many, not through one member but the body of Christ. It is through "us" and how we are seen living together, loving and serving one another that people encounter Him, not through "me" and "my ministry." The multifaceted wisdom of God needs multiple facets to be most fully displayed (Ephesians 3:10), and we encounter the fullness of Christ through His fullness, the Church (Ephesians 1:22-23).

It is through this community that people can, will and do encounter the Person who is the Way, the Truth, and the Life. Ministry happens not as a separate activity or as a "church program," rather it emerges from and within the context of everyday life.

This same backdrop, this environment in which we develop and mature spiritually, is used by God to form us. Dr. Jack Hayford, reflecting on the character and accomplishments of Winston Churchill, came to this conclusion:

"Environment ennobles, creating a sense of personal significance." (*Moments with Majesty*, p.19,1990, Multnomah Press)

He considered Churchill's early family life, his surroundings, experiences and relationships, and how this all contributed to his identity and sense of self.

God uses our community to form our personal and spiritual identity, to shape and mold our character and to imprint us with the first key elements of our destiny (this will be expanded in the rest of this section). Ultimately, community is the result of His love for us, accepting us and placing us in His family by adoption (1 Peter 2:10), and giving us significance through a role in the family business (1 Corinthians 12).

Discipleship through Relationship

Community, this shared life together in Christ, is how discipleship happens. If church is an organism and not just an organization, then discipleship is not a class we attend, it flows from life-giving relationships within the living Body of Christ. Learning both what is commanded, but also how to observe His commands (Matthew 28:18-20). If the Church, then, is an organism and not just an organization, our walk with Jesus is a relationship and not simply a system of religious belief. Our focus is not to be on a "religious" Christianity, but rather on a relationship with the person of Jesus Christ. Our relationship with Him as our King, our relationship with our community, His Body, the Church, and our relationship with those who we are called to reach out to outside the Kingdom community is what our "religion" is made up of. *It is in the context of these three relationships — Jesus, our community and those outside the Kingdom community, that we have our discipleship in Christ.*

Our Relationship with Jesus Christ

Our relationship with Jesus has many different aspects. He is the King, we are His servants. He is our Savior, we are His redeemed. He is our friend and elder brother, and we share in His inheritance as sons and daughters of His Father. But the Gospels portray one aspect of this relationship more frequently than others: *the relationship of master and teacher (Rabbi) to His disciples.* More than any other title in the Gospels, Jesus is called "master" or "teacher." His followers almost without exception are called "disciples."

Jesus spent three years ministering to those who followed Him, to those who were committed to His teachings. He ate with them, traveled with them, worshipped with them, prayed with them, ministered with them and taught them about the Kingdom of God. Of all His disciples He was closest to three men: Peter, James, and John. In the next circle of His relationships were the Twelve, beyond that the Seventy which He sent out, and beyond that the 120 that were together on the day of Pentecost. Jesus had a relationship with each of these people, each in varying degree. He taught them, ate with them, and traveled with them. It was to this small group that He devoted His most intense efforts in ministry, not the multitudes which came and went. Those who were most devoted to Him were the ones to whom He was most devoted. The casual follower may have heard His teaching from time to time, but did not have a relationship with Him.

Today, we can each have the intimacy with the Lord which Peter, James, and John had. As Christ lives within us through the person of the Holy Spirit, we can know Him as closely as we allow. We are called to be totally committed to Him after the fashion of the Three, the Twelve, the Seventy, and the 120, and not to be a "multitude" of casual followers. Continuing relationship with Him is the only path to spiritual maturity. It is only within the context of this relationship that He can make us into, and we can claim to be, His disciples.

Let us ask you some questions. Are you still a disciple of Jesus? Is He still your Master, your Rabbi? Do you still have times of sitting at His feet, learning from Him through His Word and His Spirit? Are there intimate times of worship and listening prayer? Without this ongoing intimacy, what then do you have to give away to others? If truly we are to reflect His light as we have discussed earlier, how then can we do so unless we regularly bask in it? It is essential that, even as leaders, we see ourselves first as His followers. It is essential that we do not become absorbed in task, always busy, always doing, but first embrace *being* in Christ. It is from there that we can do the Kingdom work.

Some more questions. How do you experience Christ in others? How does Jesus shape your character through interaction with others in His Body? Do you have a mentor? Who are you accountable to for your doctrine, ministry practice and way of life (in reality, not in theory)? The interdependent nature of the church places a demand for connectivity with the Body as a whole. You cannot grow and mature in Christ without receiving Him and His ministry to you through others. Don't think so? Think you can go it alone, just you and Jesus? Read on.

Our Relationship with His Body

When Jesus began His ministry, the first thing He did was to call together a band of men from every walk of life. He then began to teach these men about the Kingdom of God, and how the Kingdom was manifested in their lives by the way they related to one another. Jesus commanded His followers to love their neighbor as they loved themselves, love their enemies, to love one another as He loved them. The Gospel of the Kingdom affected not only the relationship between man and God, but also the relationship between man and man:

Honor your father and mother, and love your neighbor as yourself. (Matthew 19:19 NIV)

But I tell you who hear me: Love your enemies, do good to those who hate you, (Luke 6:27 NIV)

My command is this: Love each other as I have loved you. (John 15:12 NIV)

In the Church, we cannot have a complete relationship with the Lord without having a relationship with the others who comprise the body of Christ. Earlier we discussed the "Church as the Family of God," and how we are called into a relationship with other Christians. This is true not only because we are members of the Lord's family, but also because becoming a disciple today happens the same way it did at the time of Christ: through relationships. There are no "lone ranger" disciples or "super hero" Christians. Quite the opposite: becoming a disciple and serving the Lord as His disciple is done in the context of interacting and having relationship with other Christians. When the New Testament speaks of the church it never speaks of an individual, but of a people. The Church is not a representative person, we are a representative people.

Consequently, discipleship happens in the context of community. The sharing of life together in Christ is both the venue and methodology for training in the faith. Unlike Western training methods in use today, Jesus did not sit His disciples in a classroom environment and attempt to download information about the Father. Jesus engaged in "life-pattern teaching," where He used both *His words* and *His works* to instruct His disciples. It was not enough for them to just listen to Jesus teach, but it was just as vitally important that they observe both His character and His nature in the various situations He faced. How He reacted to the Pharisees, the woman at the well, the centurion, and all the others that He encountered on His journey was essential to their learning process.

He was the "Master," the "Rabbi," and through His life, teaching and ministry Jesus had to show them the Father (John 14:7-9). It was not enough for God to tell us about Himself — which is the core of the Old Testament. No, He had to incarnate and show us Himself. His disciples had to experience Him. They had to experience the One who was the Way, the Truth and the Life. His goal was not just having His disciples increase in knowledge about God — the Sadducees had great knowledge, but rather on seeing them enlightened in the wisdom of God. In other words, they needed to have an experiential knowledge of God through relationship with Himself, Jesus — the Incarnate Son of God. This was the way He developed His leadership team for this new community called "the Church."

Later in the New Testament, the Apostle Paul follows this same life-pattern teaching when he tells the Corinthians —

Even though you have ten thousand guardians in Christ, you do not have many fathers, for in Christ Jesus I became your father through the gospel. Therefore I urge you to imitate me. For this reason I am sending to you Timothy, my son whom I love, who is faithful in the Lord. He will remind you of my way of life in Christ Jesus, which agrees with what I teach everywhere in every church. 1 Corinthians 4:15-17

Paul reminds them again to imitate him in 1 Corinthians 11:1.

The life-pattern teaching used by Jesus in making His first disciples is still the way disciples are made today. Truth is still a Person and is known and experienced through His people. The incarnation of Christ continues now with the indwelling Holy Spirit alive and active in His Church. Being connected and in relationship in a local church is essential to being a disciple and making disciples of others.

It's not that seminars and intensives, even theological training, are bad or improper things, but if they happen outside the context of sharing life in community we are violating the very thing we are trying to re-create and extend. Unfortunately today, most of our training methods in discipleship are knowledge based and theoretical. Our theological training formats, for the most part in the West, still pull people out of organic relationships and life situations in which they are most spiritually fruitful. If we are going to repro-duce authentic, New Testament disciples, then we must be willing to rethink the methods we employ in discipleship.

Tom was once asked to attend a training event for church planters and critique the training process. The event was held in a retreat setting and was very warm and relational. However, the content of the training consisted primarily of Doctors of Theology presenting position papers to the trainees (who were mostly recent converts from the inner city.) Very high on orthodoxy, very low on orthopraxy — the nuts and bolts "how to." Lots of "what is commanded," a little bit of "how to observe." When the topic of how to disciple new converts was presented, participants in the training were given an overview of a classroom-based discipleship curriculum which was contained in a manual five inches thick! During a dialog on the use of the material, Tom asked several questions (as he is wont to do) about relational, whole-life discipleship and the environments in which discipleship could take place. The response from the instructor was firm — "discipleship happens in the classroom using the curriculum." Jesus' rabbinical approach was not on the map.

Our Relationship with a Lost World

In His parting words to His disciples in the Great Commission, Jesus said:

Then Jesus came to them and said, "All authority in heaven and on earth has been given to me. "Therefore go and make disciples of all nations, baptizing them in the name of the Father and of the Son and of the Holy Spirit, and teaching them to obey everything I have commanded you. And surely I am with you always, to the very end of the age." Matthew 28:18-20 NIV

It might surprise some Christians to know that Jesus didn't command us to "go out and get people saved," but rather that we are called to "make disciples" and "teach them to observe" (or "to do") all that He commanded us. We discussed this earlier when we looked at the Kingdom reign of God.

What is of the greatest importance in the making of disciples? As we have seen, it is the teacher having a relationship with the disciple. Our becoming disciples of Jesus has to do with spending time with Him and His Church. He spent three years in a close relationship with a small number of men. He wasn't interested in seeing people "get saved" by just praying a prayer, He was interested in investing His life in those who were becoming disciples, seeing them continue in their salvation through an ongoing relationship with Him.

If we are going to make disciples for Christ as we have been commanded to do, we must be ready to commit to having a relationship with those to whom we minister. In the case of evangelization, we must be willing to develop relationships with those in the world with whom we are called to share the Gospel. It is only in this way, in relationship, that we can be a reflective incarnation of Him. It is the only way they can ever see the Imago Dei in us;

As Jesus went on from there, he saw a man named Matthew sitting at the tax collector's booth. "Follow me," he told him, and Matthew got up and followed him. While Jesus was having dinner at Matthew's house, many tax collectors and "sinners" came and ate with him and his disciples. When the Pharisees saw this, they asked his disciples, "Why does your teacher eat with tax collectors and 'sinners'?" On hearing this, Jesus said, "It is not the healthy who need a doctor, but the sick. But go and learn what this means: 'I desire mercy, not sacrifice.' For I have not come to call the righteous, but sinners." (Matthew 9:9-13)

Jesus spent time in the homes of the outcasts of Jewish society. By doing so He brought the light of God into their lives. We are called to do the same. We cannot cloister ourselves away from those yet in the world whom Jesus is calling to be His disciples. We must be willing to have a relationship with those who don't yet know Christ, and in doing so, see them become a committed follower of Him.

Many in the Church seem to live in a "stain-glass prison," safely isolated from the messy needs of individuals right around them. This cannot be the case if we expect to see multitudes come to Christ. We must be willing to engage relationally those individuals Jesus is calling to become part of His Kingdom community. In all of Church history, there has never once been a neat, clean, orderly revival.

CHAPTER TEN

"LIVING THE 'I/THOU'"

Two Spheres of the Christian Life in Community

As we are beginning to see, all aspects of the Christian life are "I/Thou." We are never without a relational aspect, whether it be our connection to Christ, our life in community, or our relationship with those who have yet to embrace Christ. As there is an "I" and a "Thou" in the fabric of our being, these two elements of our nature create spheres of life — a *personal-life* sphere, and a *corporate-life* sphere, with corporate here meaning corpus i.e. body, and not the business connotation. The term "sphere" is used to convey an understanding of each life aspect, both personal and corporate, which is all-encompassing and three-dimensional, implying the boundaries and definition of a subject.

The personal-life sphere circumscribes that which forms a biblical framework for our individual spiritual existence, namely our **Identity**, our **Capacity**, and our **Destiny**. The corporate-life sphere bounds the three key organic organizing elements of the body/community: **Leadership**, **Health** and **Multiplication**. Both spheres exist distinct from one another as the individual is unique within the corpus; and yet the two spheres are inexorably intertwined as the body is the sum of the individuals, and which are shaped by the larger community.

Personal-life Sphere

In our **identity**, as we have been discussing, we are *Sons and Daughters* of the Most High God. We are born into His family, re-created in Imago Dei. In our character we are being developed to be *Servants* — an attitude of heart that determines our **capacity** to fulfill the God-given destiny we each have. Our **destiny** is to be a *Steward* in God's house — our role in the "family business" that we discussed earlier.

Identity: We are sons & daughters as we are born into a family

To those who accept Jesus as Christ He gives the right/power to become sons of God, born not of a human will, but born anew by God (John 1:12-13).

Our sonship comes with a spiritual genetic code from our Father in the person of the Holy Spirit. The Spirit brings Christ-likeness to us, and joins us at the heart with others in the family of God. We are being renewed in the knowledge of the Imago Dei (Colossians 3:10), imprinted on His image like ducklings following after their mother. This forms the core of our spiritual self-image. We are created in His image, become marred at birth by the fallen nature of this world, and renewed inwardly in His image at redemption. Our community, the other ducklings, also helps us form our identity, as relating with the same genetics in them we learn about our Parent.

Image is the key identity, and identity is key to successful discipleship. What is encoded in us and imprinted upon us by the Spirit of God through regeneration and by those around us through shared life in the redeemed community, is the foundation of our identity in Christ. How deeply our sonship is set in our self-perception, and if we are growing in our understanding of this reality, determines whether or not we will be fruitful in our walk with the Lord. This identity perception as a child of God will determine if we overcome when faced with the challenges of this life. Jesus knew who He was — the Son of the Father. His certainty about His identity allowed Him to face all challenges and tests presented to Him without failing one. We can only know who we are when we know Whose we are. Indeed, the pursuit of understanding our sonship in Christ is quite possibly the true issue of the Christian life, as so much of how we walk in this life is determined by the right apprehension of this understanding.

Identity is the backbone of our character, allowing us to stand in the day of evil. Much has been written on how the Lord uses His Spirit and the written Word, the Bible, to form identity in us. Not much has been written, at least of late, about how the Kingdom community — that shared life together in Christ — is used by God to form identity. The reflection of Christ, His nature, the full-ness of His grace, is seen only in His Body. Only He had the capacity to retain the fullness of God (Colossians 1:19), so now such fullness must be expressed in and through His Body.

Growing up with others of like genetics influences the development of our identity. We learn about who we are from our family. Any child locked away from other human beings will not be likely to develop a normal self-percep-tion. Any Christian locked away from God's community will not develop a proper understanding of their sonship. As discussed, the cultural ideal of the self-reliant, individualistic person who is totally self-sufficient stands in opposi-tion to this thought. We are taught we can be complete without any other person. We are imprinted with such things as "stand on your own two feet," "go it alone," "make YOUR mark on the world," and "you can do it!" (And of course, we men are taught to never stop and ask directions!) The thought of being interdependent with others, that we actually need others and what they offer us in their persons, is a cultural anathema. Saying that who we are as a person is, in part, the direct result of the shaping influence brought by the lives of others has a similar effect on us to that of fingernails being dragged across a chalk-board! It grates on us and makes us cringe.

Yet the New Testament has clear examples of how God's character, nature and His ways were demonstrated to, and imparted to, one person by the example of others with whom they lived in community. As we have said, Jesus did this as His primary method of developing His disciples. Paul reminded Timothy to reflect on Paul's pursuit of Christ — his life and teaching, and sent Timothy as an example of that way of life to the Christians in Corinth (1 Corinthians 4:15-17).

Our acceptance by the members of our community, our family, the Church is an important part of understanding our intrinsic value as recreated in the image of God (Romans 15:7). Such acceptance is essential in forming the proper self-worth understanding from God's perspective — not proud and puffed up and not degraded and broken down (Romans 12:3). Healthy self-awareness is a key component to a properly formed identity. Rejection, with which our world is filled, brings the opposite. So, life in community brings a demonstration of God's love and acceptance that is critical in the formation of one's identity as a disciple, and even healing from the wounds we may have received from being rejected by others.

Another way that community forms and informs the development of our identity is by giving us a sense of belonging. It is similar to the affect of acceptance, but goes beyond that into seeing one's self as part of a larger whole. Acceptance allows us to belong. What we belong to becomes part of who we are. Having a sense of belonging to something larger than ourselves defines us. It also inspires us to pursue growth as a person. A passion to grow, fueled by having the first elements of self-definition provided by the larger context, all but assures that any further growth will follow the same pattern provided by that context. We will become more of what we already are, more of what our environment is — just deeper, fuller, more mature and complete in its pattern. The track is set, the train will run on it until something of equal significance brings influence, and as a consequence, a possible change of direction.

This is how the Church as community influences the development of our identity. We are designed for relationship ("I/Thou"), and genetically encoded spiritually by the Trinity to only be most completed as part of a larger whole:

But you are a chosen people, a royal priesthood, a holy nation, a people belonging to God, that you may declare the praises of him who called you out of darkness into his wonderful light. Once you were not a people, but now you are the people of God; once you had not received mercy, but now you have received mercy. (1 Peter 2:9-10)

We are not chosen persons, but a chosen *people*. We are not individually *priests*, but a royal *priesthood*. We are not *persons* belonging to God, we are a people belonging to God. The "you" of the New Testament Church is plural. We are these things collectively, we are these things together. We are a spiritual nation, not a spiritual isolation.

Belonging to a community which accepts us, is the living incarnation of Christ's Body, which is living out its priesthood, living as a representative people for God — not just in words pledging to do so, but in practical works. Being part of this kind of community cannot help but shape our identity as individuals. The life, the nature of the larger group, its ways and insights, its values, doctrine and methods of spiritual practice, all become part of the individual. Again, the environment ennobles. The larger context of a shared life informs and defines who we are, who we become.

Capacity: We are servants who are being developed in our hearts

As we enter the next phase of our discussion of the personal-life sphere of a Christian, it is quite possible for one to misunderstand what we are about to say here concerning *capacity* and confuse it with the idea of *ability*. Therefore, we will seek to define it, and draw distinction up front. Capacity is related to ability, but is distinct. While ability is the power to do something, to perform some task, (like a carpenter has the ability to build a house) capacity is what allows us to "learn" how to do a thing, the aptitude for something, and consequently is the foundation of all skills. Someone who does not have the capacity (e.g. required level of mental faculties, manual dexterity) can never learn how to be a carpenter, and therefore, cannot have the capacity to build a house. They might have the mental ability to envision the house and do the math, but they might not be able to drive a nail. Or, they might be a wiz with tools, but never be able to see how it all comes together. The mental wiring and physical gifting they were endowed with, their capacity, will determine their ability.

In the spiritual context, capacity speaks of our nature, our character, our heart. That's why in the qualifications for Elders in I Timothy 3 are *capacities of being*, rather than *abilities* for *doing*. Only one is a competency — "able to teach" — and even this one will collapse if the other character qualities are not present.

The key to unleashing our God-given capacity is to take on the servant attitude of Christ Jesus (Philippians 2:1-11). The attitude of a servant puts to death the "I" and exalts the "Thou." Only servants are sons, and all sons are servants. Jesus explained this in Matthew 7:20-23:

Not everyone who says to me, 'Lord, Lord,' will enter the kingdom of heaven, but only he who does the will of my Father who is in heaven. Many will say to me on that day, 'Lord, Lord, did we not prophesy in your name, and in your name drive out demons and perform many miracles?' Then I will tell them plainly, 'I never knew you. Away from me, you evildoers!'

Jesus made it clear that mere words and great works of power were not the hallmark of God's people, but rather a submissive heart that desires to please the Father — the heart of a servant.

While we will discuss grace empowerment at length in the next section on destiny we must make mention of it here now to connect the idea of capacity together with the understanding of destiny. Even though God's enablement for service comes to us as a grace-unction of His Spirit, and therefore is unmerited, our ability to function in that empowerment (and indeed survive it) is based on our capacity. Our hearts must be truly converted, our passions under His dominion and our personal ambitions must be dead on the Cross if we hope to learn how to function most effectively in our Spiritual gifts. Expansion of the heart increases our capacity and our effectiveness within our grace empowerment. As our heart becomes more servant-motivated and less self-motivated, God is able to release more of His empowering grace to us. Without such a heart, our capacity to function most effectively within our personal, specific empowerment is diminished, and potentially fatal to what we call ministry.

Such capacity in our redeemed nature, our character and its quality, is the foundation for our destiny. It is here that capacity meets ability, as our heart has been prepared as a servant to take on the task for which we were originally created, and through which we will make our ultimate contribution in God's economy. Identity has placed us in His family, capacity has placed us in His will, and destiny now places us strategically as a resource in His cosmic undertakings. His ability to place us is related directly to what degree of faithful servanthood we have already been proven (Matthew 25:21). Where we have been tested and found faithful, we can be entrusted with more.

When we talk about this idea of capacity being a function of character, we are often asked "What does a healthy Christian look like?" Responding with some spiritual platitude would be easy, but a more developed answer might actually be useful. Health is the outcome of someone laying hold of their identity, being expanded in their capacity and being released to their destiny (more on this in a moment). For some reason, many Christians in our culture link spiritual health with someone's character being of a sterling nature. The thought is that good, moral people are spiritually healthy. But this is only true in part. As we have discussed, character development for the Christian is hugely important. A person might have the character of Christ and not make any significant contribution to the Kingdom economy. You can be a nice guy and still be absolutely worthless to God. One can do a lot in ministry activities, and be proud, arrogant, abusive, etc. — this isn't healthy either. So, here is our thought on the issue of health:

A "healthy" Christian, as a result of their on-going relationship as a disciple of Jesus Christ is someone who:

is growing in the fruit of the Spirit (Galatians 5:16-26), that is, they are growing in the character of Christ, and decreasing in the works of the flesh.

is sharing the words of Jesus with others.

is doing the works of Jesus.

is able to spiritually grow and multiply themselves by making other disciples.

A healthy Christian is one who has apprehended who they are in Christ. From that wisdom flows the life of Christ into every aspect of their existence — everything from marriage and family, to vocation and ministry. A healthy Christian is one who has experienced and continues to experience the Person who is the Way, the Truth and the Life, and reflects that person to those around them. We have included this here and a bridge to the next discussion on destiny, the last element of the personal-life sphere.

Destiny: We are stewards as we have a place of responsibility in the "family business"

Our destiny can be thought of as God's plan for us to make our ultimate contribution in His Kingdom economy as He seeks to reconcile mankind to Himself. What He has sovereignly placed in us, what spiritual gifts and natural abilities, what opportunities He has arranged for our development, all of these are "talents" which He has invested in us, empowering us for Kingdom contribution (Matthew 25:14-30). We are stewards of this grace-investment. It is not important how much we have been entrusted with, but how we undertake our stewardship. Will we be faithful or will we squander what we have been given. Here, too, community is involved in forming our destiny. Let's unpack this.

Three primary areas of our stewardship are — our life in general, our *family* and our *ministry*. The stewardship of our life encompasses our personal use of time, personal health, finances, relationships with others, etc. We learn what the biblical perspective on each is through community, and the examples of others provide the "how." Accountability to the standards set for us in Scripture in each life area is engaged relationally as well.

In the next area of destiny, the stewardship of our family, we are also shaped by the larger family around us. We learn how to love and live with a spouse, raise children in the Lord and lead a family spiritually all in the context of relationship with others who are doing so, and have done so. Indeed, our primary shaping comes from our biological/nuclear family. Yet, in our culture today many coming to Christ do so from a family context that was not Christ-centered. Broken and blended families, fatherless families, families where emotional, physical or sexual abuse were present — all these family environments can serve to impact our ability to be a steward of our family. The healthy relationships of others around us within our Christ-centered community of the Church can be used by the Lord to reform and shape our view of family and family stewardship, and to instruct us in the way of Christ-centered family life.

The last area within destiny stewardship is the stewardship we might call our ministry. The term "ministry" can be such a charged term, meaning so many different things to various people. We have been using it here as meaning the individual's contribution, as part of the large whole of the Church, to God's Kingdom economy as He works reconciliation with mankind. This, too, is formed and informed by the larger community. For the purposes of our discussion, we will look at two elements of ministry, *grace empowerment* and *assignment*, and how the community of the Body both facilitates their development and defines their implementation.

Grace is more than just God's attitude of favor towards us, it is the very substance which enables us to live for Him and serve Him. *"Grace empowerment"* is the combination of natural ability, personality and spiritual gifting that the Lord sovereignly brings together within a person to enable us to make the contribution He desires us to make to His Kingdom economy. All that we are, all that we have, comes to us as a gift from His hand, by grace. Our calling, our ability, the particular gifts of the Holy Spirit we may function in and any servant-leadership role we may play — all come as a gift; we did not earn them. It is His grace that empowers us to serve Him. As Paul said in defending his apostleship —

I am what I am by the grace of God. (1 Corinthians 15:10)

While the implantation and impartation of this grace within us and to us comes from the sovereign hand of God alone, it comes through the agency of His community. Again, even as Paul had a sovereign, personal encounter with Jesus on the Damascus Road (Acts 9), Jesus immediately directs him to Ananias and the Church in Damascus. The call for Paul to be the Lord's "chosen instrument" was a sovereign act of God (Acts 6:15), but the facilitation of it came through the Lord's people — first Ananias, then the disciples in Damascus, and then Barnabas.

As we have discussed earlier, community plays a significant role in the formation of capacity, the heart/character element that undergird the doing of ministry. It is also in the context of that shared life in community that people learn how to do ministry, how to function in spiritual gifts, how to work within the framework of the Body. Aqullia and Priscilla took Apollos in and fixed his doctrine, Paul and other elders apparently spoke the word of the Lord over young Timothy and imparted spiritual virtue through prayer. Paul notes how Timothy's faith came from his family, and knew them all well enough to use their names in the text. This all implies significant relationship. John Wimber said, "The only training for ministry is ministry," drawing his conclusion from how Jesus developed His disciples and how the Church in the Book of Acts developed people — in the Way while on the way. Those more mature in the Lord involved those coming into the Kingdom community in the serving of others, sharing the good news, praying for the sick, etc. It was on-the-job training, a development path that was more organic. It was through this means that people both discovered and developed their grace empowerment.

Grace empowerment provides the ability to undertake your God-given *assignment*. This is the role or place in the Body that God has for each of us

— our function in the family business. Paul was an Apostle to the Gentiles, Peter an Apostle to the Jews. Someone might have the grace empowerment that makes them a great Sunday School teacher or cell group leader, still someone else will be designed by God to take food to the poor. Such assignments differ from person to person, yet one thing is common — one should only serve in an assignment for which they have a grace empowerment and for which they have the capacity of heart and character to sustain.

Here the community really does play a defining role. The community as a whole and more specifically the leadership of the community, helps the person find, by the working and leading of the Holy Spirit, their fit — whatever that may be as far as ministry assignment. Using a sports analogy, the team manager and coaches decide who has the ability (grace empowerment) to play a certain position (assignment), and therefore who should play that position. The rest of the team players would affirm the choice, knowing what the team needed, seeing what the person brought to the larger whole.

In Acts 13:1-3 the leaders of the Church in Antioch discerned that the will of the Lord was for Paul and Barnabas to be sent out on a missionary journey. Please note — those being sent were part of the discernment and decision making process, but were not the sole discerners or sole deciders. The leadership team of the Antioch community was instructed to set them apart (recognize or affirm) for the work the Lord had appointed for them to do (ministry assignment). How different from our culture, where we as individuals decide what job we want to pursue, where we want to live, etc. This has been translated into the Church in our culture as well, as individual will and desire in regards to ministry service is most often the determining factor of if and how we will serve. This is the opposite of submitting to the collective wisdom of community elders, who are charged with and burdened with concern for the spiritual health and growth of the larger community.

In fact, Paul and Barnabas had only one relational crisis recorded in Scripture — over John Mark. Acts 15:36-41 shows us how they disagreed over inclusion of John Mark on a mission trip out from Antioch. Paul questions his capacity — character/heart, to undertake the trip — the ministry assignment.

More thought needs to be given by Church communities to helping people explore their grace empowerment and related ministry assignment. Giving leadership to a process that develops and validates people in ministry is key to both the fruitfulness of the individual and the Church as a whole.

Destiny — our stewardship of life, family and ministry — is given by God, but discovered in and shaped by community. Our capacity — the shaping of a servant's heart within us and our aptitude for service, is developed within the relational nexus of community. Foremost, our identity — our sonship, the re-creation of the Imago Dei within us, takes place in the context of being an interdependent part of the larger family of God, His Church. All three aspects of the personal-life sphere are influenced by Christ in His people, the Community of the King.

Corporate-life Sphere

Community's effect on the personal-life sphere of the Christian is clear. How, then, does community inform the three key organic organizing elements with the Body: **Leadership**, **Health** and **Multiplication**? In what way do people sharing life together in Christ affect the key processes of leadership development, church health and church multiplication?

Leadership Emergence in Community

Leaders for community are best formed in the environment of community — that shared life together in Christ. Drawing from what we have said through this book and applying it specifically to leadership development, the Christian leader needs to be *developed* as a *whole person*, not just *trained* for a *task*. Development doesn't happen in a classroom, it happens in the context of everyday life. The identity, capacity and destiny of a leader is formed by the community around them.

Leadership development processes must then embrace the relational life of a community, taking place in mentoring relationships as opposed to classroom settings. The rabbinical instruction model discussed earlier must be applied — "I do, you watch. I do, you help. You do, I help. You do, I watch. You do." Such mentoring does not focus only on helping the protégé acquire task-oriented skills, but on developing the whole person. Helping the protégé learn *how to live* as a disciple of Jesus in relationship, in marriage and family, in personal conduct as well as in "ministry" is essential to the development of the emerging leader.

Training in ministry praxis must be similarly engaged, as the developing leaders must be involved with the mentor in the activities they pursue in the undertaking of ministry. As we stated earlier, ministry is the training for ministry. The availability of multiple opportunities for emerging leaders to participate in is required for their fullest development. Having a loving, nurturing environment which allows experimentation in new ministries, along with grace in times of failed attempts, is essential.

Most methodologies for leadership development in the Church focus on the acquisition of Bible knowledge. While this is essential, it is incomplete. Opportunity to apply what is learned, as discussed earlier in regards to discipleship, is true here for leadership as well.

In addition to how leaders are developed, the community of the Church serves as the recognizing and commissioning entity. Acts 13:1 again is the most forthright example we may have of this, as well as Paul and "the elders" laying hands on Timothy. Trans-local authority involved in affirming leadership individuals (and warning against individuals who are false brothers), such as expressed by the Apostles, is valid as well. Specific to the role of the Apostles (e.g. James, John, Peter, Paul), we still see their connectedness to a local Church expression in some manner.

Raising Timothy: *Reproducing Shepherds*

Most of the development of pastoral ministry individuals today within our culture is done in an academic setting, whether Bible college or seminary. While there is extreme value in formal theological education, the current majority format of separating people from the community environment for four to seven years is at best debilitating the Body of Christ, and at worst, perverting into something the Church is not meant to be — an institution.

Removing someone from the community context for training negates the effects of community in the formative process. It destroys the natural evangelistic and pastoral relationships the individual has organically and intuitively developed. Again, as we have seen earlier, ministry development happens best when living in community. Pastors need to be raised up organically within the context of an active, vibrant Church, having reproduced within them both the life of the community and the skills for ministry.

There are many opportunities today to access theological education by extension, whether it is through a regional school or seminar, online or through distance learning. All such opportunities should be pursued before the person leaves the context of their fruitfulness.

Pastoral ministry is not a profession, it is an organic role as part of a larger organic whole. It is spiritual parenthood, eldership within a community that has known and validated the life and ministry of the leader. It can be done with excellence and professional standards, but it must never become a "job." Validation in ministry comes not from degrees earned, but from fruit produced. Ministry as a profession is a cultural dynamic, not a New Testament reality.

Compensating someone who does pastoral ministry is clearly supported in the New Testament, so we are not suggesting otherwise. The community served should care for the financial needs of the person accordingly. It is the attitude of the heart of which we are speaking. If we are to be professional anything, it would be professional servants. The way to test your own heart — "Would you still be the pastor of these people if you did not get paid?" — will tell you whether you, in your heart, are a "professional" or a spiritual parent. Compensation is fine as long as the heart remains linked to the organic reality of the Church as family and community, and not as an employer or customer.

Health and Fruitfulness within the Community

Honestly, this is the easiest topic within the book to address as there already exists within the Church an understanding of the organic nature of the Church and how that relates to the health of the Body. Natural Church Development (NCD), the work of Christian Schwarz of the Institute for Natural Church Development, is the best understanding to date of the organic nature of the church and how it relates to health and growth. (He has authored a book on NCD, which we highly recommend.) We will not take the time to recap his research into the Church and what makes it grow. Instead we will offer a brief summary, as it relates to the organic nature of the Church. NCD is not a church growth program, but rather an organic paradigm of the Church as a living thing, the Body of Christ.

In summary, what NCD illuminates is:

The church is an organic, living thing, and not an institution,

That growth is a function of health, not more effort,

That Jesus is building His church, and that He has designed the Church to grow all by itself (Matthew 16:18, mark 4:26-29),

That role of leadership is to partner with what God is already at work doing, and remove the obstacles to growth that exist in a Church,

And in that partnership, God has reserved for us things which He will not do; and reserved for Himself things which we cannot do. (1 Corinthians 3:6-9)

Community is reflected within the NCD Quality Characteristics

Empowering leadership — essential for community

Gift-oriented ministry — the organic self-organization of the Body (1 Corinthians 12)

Passionate spirituality — the soul of community

Functional Structures — the "wineskin" which holds the community together

Inspiring worship service — the large group gathering of the community — "in the temple"

Holistic small groups — living out the "one another's" of the New Testament

Need-oriented evangelism — community reflecting Jesus to the world

Loving Relationships — the foundation of community

Indeed, looking back at our values for the church as expressed in Acts 2:42-47 we see most, if not all, of these characteristics present in the life of the early Church community.

Community is reflected in NCD Biotic Principles

Interdependence — at the core of community

Multiplication — the goal of community

Energy transformation — conflict resolution within community brings new life

Multi-usage — community is more flexible than institution, and allows for multi-usage

Symbiosis — the Spirit in the Church produces incarnational community

Functionality — the practicality of community — relationship allows for the practical implementation of Christ's teachings.

The biotic principles are not a program, but a paradigm of HOW the Church should function. They link together the key understanding of the Church as community and how the church achieves health and becomes fruitful. You cannot live the biotic principles without living in community.

Church Multiplication In Community — The Antioch Example

Looking once again to the example of the Church in Antioch, specifically in Acts 13:1-3, we see the principle of multiplication was already at work on the Church:

In the church at Antioch there were prophets and teachers: Barnabas, Simeon called Niger, Lucius of Cyrene, Manaen (who had been brought up with Herod the tetrarch) and Saul. While they were worshiping the Lord and

*fasting, the Holy Spirit said, "Set apart for me Barnabas and Saul for the work
to which I have called them." So after they had fasted and prayed, they placed
their hands on them and sent them off.*

What can we see about church multiplication? (A whole book could be
written on this subject alone — we will just overview it here.)

At some point previous to this moment they had collectively embraced
the Spirit's desire for Kingdom expansion. They had to be open to it for it to
be within the realm of their thinking concerning Barnabas and Paul.

There is the intentional reproduction of their community as a means of
spreading the Gospel and thereby extending the Kingdom. Life giving birth to
life. The Apostles were not just sowing the seeds of a message, they were
sowing seeds of a way of life.

They employed a method to seek God and fulfill their intention: Prayer
and fasting in search of God's will, with these outcomes realized:

Leadership call affirmed and sanctioned as a result

Team deployed to fulfill the mission — John added

A method was used: going first to the synagogues

Paul and Barnabas did not go out on their own to do their will. They were
sent from a community to form a new community in each of the places they
visited — a community of sons and daughters of the Most High, an extension
of God's family in the earth. To us, community formation in church planting is
an afterthought, as we lack community within our culture. We regard it as
something important but not essential. To them it was a given as they
assumed community was at the core of the Church, because it was all about
relating to God and to others. The "I/Thou" was in the mission work of this
early mission team.

Just as the personal-life sphere is influenced and formed by living life
together in Christ community — the corporate-life sphere of the Body — is
impacted as well. The Church cannot be the Church and fulfill its purpose for
existence unless it allows the community of the Trinity to be formed within it,
and that cannot occur unless we as individuals understand ourselves as His
children, part of His family. Then we can become the Imago Dei, and reflect
Christ to the world around us. If revival is to come, if our culture is to be
turned and people by the thousands brought into the Kingdom of God, we
will not need more plans, programs or crusades; we will need simply for the
Church to become the community of the King, the family of God.

CONCLUSION

"COMMUNITY IN ETERNITY"

Where does all this lead? Well, unlike our *Lord of the Rings* example where at the end of the story the Fellowship is dissolved in a bitter-sweet parting, there is no such sundering of the Fellowship of the Cross. We will enjoy our community — indeed our communion with the Lord — forever. That is where all this leads — not to a journey's end — but to an everlasting adventure together in Him:

After this I looked and there before me was a great multitude that no one could count, from every nation, tribe, people and language, standing before the throne and in front of the Lamb. They were wearing white robes and were holding palm branches in their hands. And they cried out in a loud voice: "Salvation belongs to our God, who sits on the throne, and to the Lamb." (Revelation 7:9-10)

Then I saw a new heaven and a new earth, for the first heaven and the first earth had passed away, and there was no longer any sea. I saw the Holy City, the new Jerusalem, coming down out of heaven from God, prepared as a bride beautifully dressed for her husband. And I heard a loud voice from the throne saying, "Now the dwelling of God is with men, and he will live with them. They will be his people, and God himself will be with them and be their God. He will wipe every tear from their eyes. There will be no more death or mourning or crying or pain, for the old order of things has passed away.

He who was seated on the throne said, "I am making everything new!

(Revelation 21:1-5a)

This New Testament Trilogy of *Our God, Ourselves* and *Our Community* outlasts time. What we have written of here, and hope that you work towards in your own life, ministry and church is but a dim reflection of that which is yet to come — the Kingdom community realized in its fullness — God with His people, and His people as one. This Trilogy is meant to spur you onward, to press deeper into God, to stir a holy discontent with the status quo of the

Church in our culture. It is not exhaustive in addressing the huge topics discussed — rather, it is just a part of that journey of rediscovery the Lord wishes to lead you on. But don't just think about it, live it. God's Kingdom community lasts forever — *and you and your church can begin living that community right now.*

EPILOGUE I

THE ADVENTURE BEGINS

One good thing that you have in your future is the fact that no one will ever make this Trilogy into a movie. No matter how amazing the special effects were, it would still be a flop. Why? Because it is not something, like an epic saga, that stands forth on its own. No, in fact, what it portrays is the drama of how the Person who is the Way, the Truth and the Life expresses Himself through the Church — it is still all a framework of understanding. It only becomes an epic adventure when life — your life, and the life of the Church you are part of — is added to the understanding of the Church given here. Then it becomes alive, then it becomes organic, then it becomes truly real in the experiential sense. It is then that Trilogy becomes more than information, more than knowledge — it becomes some part of the wisdom of the way of God, something alive. It becomes organic when you take it from these pages and apply it. Then it becomes of use to you, and then it has real value.

Here are some first steps to consider in implementing what you have learned here:

First, read it all again. Make sure you really get it before you try to do it.

Second, realize this is not a church program, but the rediscovery of a way of life — the church as a community, a shared life together in Christ. Resist efforts to try to graft it into your current ecclesiological paradigm. It won't work unless the genetics of your community are already really close to what is portrayed here. Reaction to foreign genetic material can cause organs to fail, and even death. Program-based church and organic-relationship community are incompatible.

Take your notes from your first two readings and form a list of outcomes you want to see reflected in the community you serve.

Develop a one-to-two year teaching plan to communicate and inculcate in your church the ideas presented in Trilogy.

Implement the Rabbinical/Socratic teaching model, focusing on developing people, not just training them.

Define your relationships. Like Jesus did, determine who are your three, your twelve and your seventy-two. Then begin to live life together. Incarnate it for them.

Restructure leadership and ministry systems around these definitions.

Transition (read: "kill slowly and silently") the cultural elements of the church you serve that are not rooted in the New Testament understanding of Church as community.

Check the Trilogy web section of the Praxis website (www.praxiscenter.org) often for new developmental tools related to Trilogy currently under development to help you with discipleship, leadership development, training pastors, and church multiplication.

Bathe everything you do in prayer, asking the Lord to guide you and enlighten those whom you lead.

May the Lord bless you, and the community you lead, on your journey of rediscovery!

EPILOGUE II

THE ALTERNATIVE RESPONSE

Well, O.K. — so you don't really want to work all that hard at this church thing anyway. Hey, why grow and change, right? Too much work. We've crafted an alternative response to this book in this second Epilogue. So, if the ten steps we just laid out are overwhelming, go with "Plan B:"

Instead of re-reading this book, just shred it, because you can only handle so much theology anyway.

Instead of spiritual "gene therapy" for your church, get some of the new sermon-enhancing steroids.

Instead of listing outcomes to work towards, just tell the people what you want them to do. You know what's best, right?

Instead of developing a two-year preaching plan from Trilogy, just repeat "40 Days of Purpose" 15 times in a row. (Hey Rick, we love ya, man!)

Instead of the Socratic/rabbinical method of teaching, use the "drill sergeant" methodology and shout orders at people.

Instead of defining your relationships like Jesus did, simply isolate yourself from people and only come out on Sundays.

Restructure leadership and ministry systems around yourself. If you can't do it, no one can; and no one can do it as good as you. Face it, God would be hurting without you.

Why wait? Change everything now! Kill today those things/systems/ministry programs in your church that really tick you off.

Don't bother visiting www.praxiscenter.org, as you already have all the tools you need to single-handedly conquer the world for Jesus.

Tell God everything you are going to do and ask Him to bless it.

May you become famous and wealthy as you tell everyone how to do it! (Remember us when you come into your kingdom.)

If this doesn't work, try the steps suggested in Epilogue I.

(Please forgive us, but if you wrote this much theology, you'd feel like this too!)

A New Testament Trilogy R.E.A.D. Questions

Each chapter in this book will have a series of questions. Using the acronym R.E.A.D., these questions will help you **R**eflect, **E**valuate, **A**djust and **D**o.

Wisdom in the Holy Spirit comes from reflecting on biblical truth. Evaluation allows you to look at your current ministry praxis in light of a biblical world view. This allows you to adjust your life and ministry accordingly (read: repent). Based on the Spirit-led adjustment, you can now do or implement life and ministry based on the new realities you have become aware of.

The questions at the end of each chapter are framed within the context that the "personal-life sphere" encompasses everything of our life — our identify, capacity and destiny in Christ. However, we will use an artificial construct of "life and ministry practice" to help you self-evaluate within the broader prevalent thinking in the Western Church. Normally, we would not promote such dichotomous thinking, as we are not modalists. Like the human brain which has two hemispheres, right and left, and yet is one brain, we will bisect the person (life and ministry practice), even though they are one.

Chapter One R.E.A.D. Questions — "God is One"

R – Based on your *reflection*, list the three major things that the Holy Spirit spoke to your heart regarding your life and ministry practice.

How is your theology autobiographical?

What is your personal experience with the "I/Thou?" Describe your most recent personal encounter with God. How long ago was it?

E – Based on the new awareness that you have gained, how would you *evaluate* your current life and ministry practices?

Describe your earthly father and your Heavenly Father. How are they the same and not the same?

Are you having daily encounters with God? Are they fulfilling?

A – What do you need to *adjust* on each of the above?

D – What <u>will</u> you *do* about it?

Chapter Two R.E.A.D. Questions — "God is Trinity: a Community"

R – Based on your *reflection*, list the three major things that the Holy Spirit spoke to your heart regarding your life and ministry practice.

In what way does God as Trinity impact your life and ministry?

E – Based on the new awareness that you have gained, how would you *evaluate* your current life and ministry practices?

If life (ministry) flows from who we are (being in Christ), so then how does life flow from you to others? See 2 Corinthians 1:4 — What is the comfort you have received?

Read John 17:21. How does your current life and ministry practice reflect the unity and interdependence of the Trinity? Who surrounds you? Who are you giving life to and who are you receiving life from?

A – What do you need to *adjust*?

Priorities?

Schedule?

Relationships?

Paradigm of life?

Philosophy of ministry?

D – What will you *do* about it?

Chapter Three R.E.A.D. Questions — "God is Love"

R – Based on your *reflection*, list the three major things that the Holy Spirit spoke to your heart regarding your life and ministry practice.

How does the love in the Trinity reflected in your relationships? (Love for God, self and others.)

E – Based on the new awareness that you have gained, how would you *evaluate* your current life and ministry practices?

How is your life consistent with John 13:34-35?

How is your life and ministry reflective of God's love in justice, truth and grace?

A – What do you need to *adjust*?

D – What will you *do* about it?

Chapter Four R.E.A.D. Questions — "The Creation of Humankind"

R – Reflect on Romans 12:4-5. Based on your *reflection*, list the three major things that the Holy Spirit spoke to your heart regarding your life and ministry practice.

If creation of humankind begins with and flows from community, how does your life reflect community?

If we are built to be in community, why do we choose to isolate ourselves from others?

How has this chapter broadened your understanding of koinonia?

What is your best personal example of experiencing this level of koinonia?

E – Based on the new awareness that you have gained, how would you *evaluate* your current life and ministry practices? How does your life align with that passage?

How are you connected to the Head, who is Christ?

How are you connected to others, and how are others connected to you?

Who is your "Fellowship of the Cross?"

Evaluate Mr. Spock's maxim and apply it to the church: "The needs of the many outweigh the needs of the few, or the one."

A – What do you need to *adjust*?

D – What will you *do* about it?

Chapter Five R.E.A.D. Questions — "Imago Dei: Life Father, like Son"

R – Based on your *reflection*, list the three major things that the Holy Spirit spoke to your heart regarding your life and ministry practice.

What does it mean to be created in the Imago Dei?

How does your understanding of being created in God's image affect your self perception?

E – Based on the new awareness that you have gained, how would you *evaluate* your current life and ministry practices?

If we are dependent beings, how are you living out your dependency on God? (See Matthew 5:3)

A – What do you need to *adjust*?

D – What <u>will</u> you *do* about it?

Chapter Six R.E.A.D. Questions — "How Humankind Comes to Know God"

R – Based on your *reflection*, list the three major things that the Holy Spirit spoke to your heart regarding your life and ministry practice.

How did God-awareness first come into your heart?

Describe how you have experienced Romans 8:16?

E – Based on the new awareness that you have gained, how would you *evaluate* your current life and ministry practices?

Evaluate your faith — is it assent, *trust or faithfulness*?

Why do we seek more knowledge and information when we already know what we are to do?

A – What do you need to *adjust*?

D – What <u>will</u> you *do* about it?

Chapter Seven R.E.A.D. Questions — "The Reign of God: His Kingdom Community"

R – Based on your *reflection*, list the three major things that the Holy Spirit spoke to your heart regarding your life and ministry practice.

How are you putting aside selfish ambition as you take up the Cross daily?

E – Based on the new awareness that you have gained, how would you *evaluate* your current life and ministry practices?

In relation to the elements of Kingdom community, how are you living out *incarnation*, *proclamation* and *demonstration*?

A – What do you need to *adjust*?

D – What <u>will</u> you *do* about it?

Chapter Eight R.E.A.D. Questions — "The Church as a Family"

R – Based on your *reflection*, list the three major things that the Holy Spirit spoke to your heart regarding your life and ministry practice.

What is your understanding of the family of God?

E – Based on the new awareness that you have gained, how would you *evaluate* your current life and ministry practices?

Where have you allowed the organizational aspects of "church" to overwhelm its organic nature?

In what ways are you living out interdependence with others in the Body of Christ?

Reflect on Ephesians 4:3-6. If God is one, and the church which is made in His image is one, and we are unified, what then are you doing to maintain or keep the unity of the Body?

A – What do you need to *adjust*?

D – What <u>will</u> you *do* about it?

Chapter Nine R.E.A.D. Questions — "The Church as Community"

R – Based on your *reflection*, list the three major things that the Holy Spirit spoke to your heart regarding your life and ministry practice.

Reflect on your experience of a shared life together in Christ.

What person in your life has had the greatest impact on you as a disciple?

E – Based on the new awareness that you have gained, how would you *evaluate* your current life and ministry practices?

Read Acts 2:42-47. Evaluate your current experience of community with that of the early church.

How do people encounter Christ in a transformational way in the everyday life of your community?

Who are you in relationship with that is forming you as a disciple? Who are you forming?

A – What do you need to *adjust*?

D – What will you *do* about it?

Chapter Ten — "Living the 'I/Thou'"

R – Based on your *reflection*, list the three major things that the Holy Spirit spoke to your heart regarding your life and ministry practice.

What does it mean to be a son/daughter of God? How does this affect your daily life?

What is your grace?

E – Based on the new awareness that you have gained, how would you *evaluate* your current life and ministry practices?

How are you doing as a: *son/daughter, servant* and *steward*?

A – What do you need to *adjust*?

D – What will you *do* about it?